**European Monetary
Integration**

European Monetary Integration

edited by
Hans-Werner Sinn,
Mika Widgrén, and
Marko Köthenbürger

CESifo Seminar Series

The MIT Press
Cambridge, Massachusetts
London, England

This book was set in Palatino by Interactive Composition Corporation and was printed and bound in the United States of America.

Library of Congress Cataloging-in-Publication Data

European monetary integration/edited by Hans-Werner Sinn, Mika Widgrén, and Marko Köthenbürger.
p. cm. — (CESifo seminar series)
Includes index.
ISBN 0-262-19499-6 (alk. paper)
1. Monetary unions—European Union countries. 2. Economic and Monetary Union.
3. European Union countries—Economic integration I. Sinn, Hans-Werner. II. Widgrén, Mika. III. Köthenbürger, Marko. IV. Series.

HG3894.E93 2004
332.4'94—dc22

2003061499

10 9 8 7 6 5 4 3 2 1

Contents

Contributors

Philippe Bacchetta
Study Center Gerzensee
PO Box 21
3115 Gerzensee
Switzerland
tel: +41 31 7803101
fax: +41 31 7803100
email: *phbacchetta@szgerzensee.ch*

Helge Berger
Department of Economics
Free University Berlin
Boltzmannstrasse 20
14195 Berlin
Germany
email: *hberger@wiwiss.fu-berlin.de*

Fabrizio Coricelli
University of Siena
Department of Economics
Piazza San Francesco 7
53100 Siena
Italy
tel: +39 0577 232799
fax: +39 0577 232661
email: *coricelli@unisi.it*

Alex Cukierman
Tel-Aviv University
Berglas School of Economics
69978 Tel-Aviv
Israel
tel: +972 3 6409 909
fax: +972 3 6409 908
email: *alexcuk@post.tau.ac.il*

Alberto Dalmazzo
University of Siena
Department of Economics
Piazza San Francesco 7
53100 Siena
Italy
tel: +39 0577 232620
fax: +39 0577 232661
email: *dalmazzo@unisi.it*

Jakob de Haan
University of Groningen
Department of Economics
PO Box 800
9700 AV, Groningen
Netherlands
tel: +31 50 3633706
fax: +31 50 3633720
email: *j.de.haan@eco.rug.nl*

Jørgen Elmeskov
OECD
2, Rue André Pascal
75775 Paris Cedex 16
France
tel: +33 1 45247602
email: *jorgen.elmeskov@oecd.org*

Holger Feist
McKinsey
Prinzregentenstrasse 22
80538 Munich
Germany
email: *Holger_Feist@mckinsey.com*

Daniel Gros
Centre for European Policy
Studies
Department of Economics
Place du Congrès 1
1000 Brussels
Belgium
tel: +32 2 229 39 11
fax: +32 2 219 41 51
email: *daniel.gros@ceps.be*

Carsten Hefeker
HWWA—Institute of
International Economics
Neuer Jungfernstieg 21
20347 Hamburg
Germany
tel: +49-40-42834-346/7
fax: +49-40-42834-451
email: *Carsten.Hefeker@hwwa.de*

Gerhard Illing
Ludwig-Maximilians University
München
Department of Economics
Ludwigstraße 28 RGb
80539 Munich
Germany

tel: +49-89-2180 2126
fax: +49-89-2180 13521
email:
gerhard.illing@lrz.uni-muenchen.de

Robert Inklaar
University of Groningen
Department of Economics
PO Box 800
9700 AV, Groningen
Netherlands
email: *R.C.Inklaar@eco.rug.nl*

Svend E. Hougaard Jensen
Centre for Economic and
Business Research
Langelinie Alle 17
2100 Copenhagen Ø
Denmark
tel: +45 3546 6537
fax: +45 3546 6201
email: *shj@efs.dk*

Erkki Koskela
University of Helsinki
Department of Economics
Arkadiankatu 7
PO Box 17
00014 Helsinki
Finland
tel: +358 9 1918894
fax: +358 9 1918877
email: *erkki.koskela@helsinki.fi*

Christopher A. Sims
Princeton University
Department of Economics
104 Fisher Hall
Princeton, NJ 08544-1021
tel: +1 609 2584033
fax: +1 609 2586419
email: *sims@princeton.edu*

Hans-Werner Sinn
CESifo
Poschingerstraße 5
80679 Munich
Germany
tel: +49 89 9224 1410
fax: +49 89 9224 1409
email: *sinn@cesifo.de*

Jouko Vilmunen
Bank of Finland
PO Box 160
Fin-00101 Helsinki
Finland
tel: +358-9-183 2594
fax: +358-9-183 2560
email: *jouko.vilmunen@bof.fi*

Mika Widgrén
Turku School of Economics and
Business Administration
Economics Department
Room 325
Rehtorinpellonkatu 3
20500 Turku
Finland
tel: +358 2 3383337
fax: +358 2 3383302
email: *mika.widgren@tukkk.fi*

Series Foreword

This book is part of the CESifo Seminar Series in Economic Policy, which aims to cover topical policy issues in economics from a largely European perspective. The books in this series are the products of the papers presented and discussed at seminars hosted by CESifo, an international research network of renowned economists supported jointly by the Center for Economic Studies at Ludwig-Maximilians-Universität, Munich, and the Ifo Institute for Economic Research. All publications in this series have been carefully selected and refereed by members of the CESifo research network.

Introduction

European monetary integration is one of the most far-reaching, real world experiments in monetary policy to date. On January 1, 1999, the final stage of the European Economic and Monetary Union (EMU) commenced with the irrevocable fixing of the exchange rates of the eleven member state currencies and with the conduct of a single monetary policy under the responsibility of the European Central Bank (ECB). The euro was virtually introduced at that date and on January 1, 2002, the new currency was introduced physically. There are currently twelve member countries, and there will be many more when the eastern European countries which become part of the EU in 2004 also join the monetary union. The euro will then cover a larger economy than the dollar.

Despite its apparent popularity, the success of EMU is not self-evident. Notably the prerequisite posed by Mundell's theory of optimum currency areas does not appear to be satisfied. Business cycles in member countries are still asymmetric, and the economies of Europe are still in very different stages of development, making it difficult for the ECB to formulate an appropriately uniform monetary policy. Moreover the decision-making structure within the ECB council is guided by the principle of "one country, one vote," which gives small countries a large political power relative to their economic weight. This could magnify the costs of a uniform monetary strategy and call for more academic policy advice in order to make EMU a success.

The first three chapters of this volume especially address the asymmetry problems in EMU. Fabrizio Coricelli, Alex Cukierman, and Alberto Dalmazzo analyze the question of whether the commonly presumed trade-off between inflation and conservativeness of the central bank still holds if a uniform monetary policy is imposed on asymmetric countries where asymmetry originates from different degrees of labor and product market rigidities. While, as expected, uniformity induces a welfare loss, each country's welfare increases as the central bank becomes more inflation averse. Significantly the core Rogoff-type trade-off between inflation and conservativeness continues to be applicable. The finding has particular relevance for the EMU because labor and product market imperfections differ between countries, although they are severe everywhere. Erkki Koskela calls for enriching the model in two ways. First, the impact of economic integration on product market competition should be modeled explicitly. Second, Koskela suggests disentangling the impact of conservativeness and market imperfections on the evolution of European unemployment more thoroughly by adopting a dynamic framework designed to capture the unemployment hysteresis prevailing in the EMU.

In the second chapter, Daniel Gros and Carsten Hefeker assess the costs of a uniform ECB policy. When "one size does not fit all," which policy objective should underlie monetary policy? The question posed by the authors is whether, for example, the Spanish unemployment figure should enter the ECB decision making as one element in calculating EU-wide averages or whether the welfare loss in Spain inflicted by unemployment should directly guide European monetary policy. Gros and Hefeker show that EU welfare tends to improve if the ECB considers the average of national welfare losses instead of focusing on a policy objective based on average inflation and unemployment rates. The finding casts doubt on the current practice of holding the ECB accountable for the average inflation performance in the entire euro area. Jørgen Elmeskov is skeptical about the political feasibility of a change in the ECB's objective function, and he sees merits in the simplicity of the present ECB approach. He also criticizes the authors' assumption of a uniform inflation rate in the EMU, which excludes the possibility of a negative correlation between inflation and unemployment. If there is such a negative correlation, he maintains, the problem pointed out by Gros and Hefeker loses its importance.

Looking into the "black box" of central bank decision making, Helge Berger, Jacob DeHaan, and Robert Inklaar identify a bias in voting power in the ECB council toward small member countries. Since business cycles do not tend to be synchronized within the EMU, the asymmetry between voting power and economic power will imply that ECB policy has negative real effects in large countries. Berger, DeHaan, and Inklaar thereby highlight a problem inherent in the ECB constitution that will gain greater relevance in the course of European enlargement during which small countries, with their presumably high inflation rates during the economic transition process, join EMU. In his comments Mika Widgrén calls for adding institutional aspects of ECB decision making to the analysis. In addition he argues that spatial voting models could be used to assess the severity of the identified bias more explicitly.

An equally important aspect of European central banking, namely the relation between the ECB and national fiscal authorities created by the distribution of seignorage revenues, is taken up in the chapters by Christopher Sims, and Hans-Werner Sinn and Holger Feist. Sims points to a necessary limitation on the level of ECB independence. Though formally politically independent in its pursuit of price stability, the ECB implicitly faces a nonnegativity constraint on seignorage revenues that might indirectly hamper monetary policy. He concludes that the ECB's current monetary policy stance of stabilizing the quantity of money besides inflation targeting can be interpreted as a best response to the seignorage constraint. Targeting the quantity of money rather than the inflation rate has the advantage of reducing the risk of running out of reserves and violating the seignorage constraint. The discussant Svend Jensen points to a possible wider interpretation of the results. In his opinion Sims's analysis might also lay a theoretical foundation for the Stability and Growth Pact, which, by easing potential fiscal pressures on the ECB, allows the ECB to pursue its primary objective of achieving price stability. However, as an overall assessment Jensen is skeptical concerning the practical relevance of the issue raised by Sims.

Hans-Werner Sinn and Holger Feist predict a significant redistribution of seignorage income among EMU members. The redistribution results from the fact that the interest income a central bank contributes to the ECB is proportional to the monetary base it brought into the union, while its interest rebates from the ECB are proportional to country size. As a large fraction of the German monetary base circulated in eastern Europe and as the peseta was widely used for the Spanish black market purposes, Germany and Spain incurred substantial fiscal losses from the introduction of the euro. As a policy conclusion Sinn and Feist argue that the unintended redistributive consequences call for a revision of the Maastricht Treaty. In his discussion Jouko Vilmunen doubts whether this redistribution was indeed unforeseen. When negotiating the treaty all relevant information was available, suggesting, for instance, that Germany rationally considered the wealth transfer as a price for the benefits of establishing the monetary union. If indeed unforeseen, Vilmunen views side-payments as a better solution to this asymmetry than renegotiating the Maastricht Treaty.

The last chapter, by Gerhard Illing, highlights the interaction between ECB monetary policy and financial market behavior, in particular, asset price dynamics. The question received tremendous attention right after the establishment of the ECB, when stock prices increased significantly, and recommendations to address the bubble through ECB policy were voiced. In particular, Illing's contribution stresses the importance of expectations in financial markets. He argues that a lender-of-last-resort commitment by a central bank might inflate asset prices. Such a commitment can be rationalized by concerns about a disruption of financial intermediation in the course of a financial crisis. The central bank may find it desirable to inject liquidity to save firms and banks, thereby triggering asset price bubbles. In his comments Philippe Bacchetta wonders whether the proposed mechanism for creating bubbles can explain the ever-rising share prices of the late 1990s. He furthermore calls for more information on the transmission channel of monetary policy.

In sum, these chapters attempt to shed some light on the many difficult policy issues that have to be solved if the European experiment of introducing the euro is to enter the history books as a success story.

I

Asymmetries and ECB Policy

1

Economic Performance and Stabilization Policy in a Monetary Union with Imperfect Labor and Goods' Markets

Fabrizio Coricelli,
Alex Cukierman, and
Alberto Dalmazzo

1.1 Introduction

In this chapter we propose a framework for the analysis of the effects of institutions on economic performance in a monetary union in the presence of unionized labor markets and monopolistically competitive, price-setting firms. The development of such a framework is motivated by the creation of the European Monetary Union (EMU), by the observation that European labor markets are largely unionized with different degrees of centralization in wage bargaining (CWB) across member countries of the Monetary Union (MU), and by the belief that the paradigm of monopolistically competitive, price-setting firms provides a better description of reality than that of perfectly competitive firms.

The chapter has three main objectives. The first is to analyze the effects of country size and the degree of centralization of wage bargaining across countries on the MU-wide, as well as on country-specific, economic performance in the presence of a single unified monetary policy. The second is to analyze the effect of the level of conservativeness of the common central bank on union wide, as well as on country specific, average economic performance. The third is to examine how those factors (country size, centralization of wage bargaining and central bank conservativeness) are likely to affect stabilization policy by the common central bank (CB) in the face of common, as well as of differential, demand and productivity shocks.

By now it is well accepted that central bank conservativeness (CBC) is negatively related to inflation. Recent literature has additionally discovered that in the presence of large wage setters, the level of CBC also affects real economic activity even if unions are not averse to inflation, and that the magnitude of those real effects depends on the structure of wage bargaining (Cukierman and Lippi 1999; Soskice and Iversen 2000; Lippi 1999; Coricelli, Cukierman, and Dalmazzo 2000).[1]

The creation of EMU has raised the effective CBC for most countries that have joined the Monetary Union. As CBC has real effects, one may question whether or not a reform of monetary policy-making institutions is desirable. The framework we propose makes it possible to identify some factors that affect this issue. In particular, we show that a high level of CBC is associated with both lower inflation and lower unemployment in the aggregate. However, when in the presence of shocks a stabilization policy is desirable, we are faced with the familiar Rogoff (1985) type trade-off between average economic performance and stabilization. Product market competition and wage-bargaining institutions also play a fundamental role in the determination of inflation and of unemployment in the MU. We show that higher CWB and higher product market competition in the MU lowers the expected value of inflation and the MU wide rate of unemployment.

In addition to the aggregate performance of the MU, in the performances of the member countries we find that a higher level of CBC is associated with both lower inflation and lower unemployment at the country level. However, because the countries in the MU differ in size and in the degree of centralization in wage bargaining (CWB), a common monetary policy can have different effects on the economic performances of the different countries even in the absence of shocks (a recent survey appears in Franzese 2000). As we will show below, the framework we use makes it possible to analyze the different impacts of a common monetary policy.[2] Other things being the same, the countries in the MU that possess relatively more centralized wage-bargaining systems are more competitive in foreign trade within the union and enjoy lower rates of unemployment. Similar conclusions hold for relatively larger countries. Basically these results are a direct consequence of the fact that unions in larger countries with more centralized wage-bargaining systems internalize a larger fraction of the impact of their actions on employment, and this moderates their wage demands.

In the chapter we also show that independently of the level of conservativeness, the CB of the MU fully offsets an appropriately weighted average of the demand shocks of the individual countries. Although optimal at the level of the entire MU, a policy that offsets all MU-wide demand shocks does not fully stabilize the effects of different demand shocks on individual countries' rates of unemployment. Unlike demand shocks, central bank conservativeness affects the CB's reaction to

MU-wide productivity shocks. An interesting result of the chapter is that a more conservative CB reacts more strongly to supply shocks in order to stabilize inflation. This result is consistent with recent time series evidence on conservativenes and activism in Germany presented by Berger and Woitek (1999).

Section 1.2 presents the basic building blocks of the model and derives its equilibrium solution. The interactions among unions, the CB, and firms are presented as a three-stage game. The players are the (nominal) wage-setting unions, a CB that picks the money supply in the MU, and a large number of monopolistically competitive, price-setting firms in the countries of the MU. Section 1.3 considers the effects of country size and other institutional parameters, like product market competitivenes, CWB, and CBC, on the expected economic performance at both the MU and the individual country levels. Section 1.4 discusses the implications of optimal stabilization of shocks at the level of the MU for CB activism, realized inflation, MU-wide unemployment, country-specific rates of unemployment, and relative competitiveness. This is followed by concluding remarks.

1.2 The Model

The analytical framework extends the closed economy model in Coricelli, Cukierman, and Dalmazzo (2000; henceforth CCD 2000) by explicitly recognizing open economy interactions and the role of productivity and demand shocks. The monetary union is composed of two countries. In each country there is a continuum of monopolistically competitive firms each producing a single differentiated product. The labor force in each country is divided into a number of equal-sized labor unions that manage the country's entire labor force. Firms are evenly distributed over the unit interval, and their total mass is one. A fraction, s_1, of firms is located in country 1 and the remainder ($s_2 = 1 - s_1$) is located in country 2.

Each union in each country organizes a labor pool of size $1/n_c$ where n_c is the number of unions in country c, with $c = 1, 2$. As a consequence s_c also represents the share of country c in the combined labor force of the monetary union. An equal quantity, L_0, of workers is attached to each firm and works only if the union in charge signs a labor contract with the firm. For convenience, and without loss of generality, the firms in country c are indexed so that all firms whose labor force is represented by union i are located in the contiguous subinterval

$(\frac{i}{n_c}s_c, \frac{i+1}{n_c}s_c)$ of the interval of length s_c, where $i = 0, 1, \ldots, n_c - 1$. In both countries the firms own a production technology that exhibits decreasing returns to scale to labor input and is subject to a country-specific productivity shock Z_c, whose logarithm has an expected value of zero:

$$Y_{ij}^c = L_{ij}^\alpha \cdot Z_c, \qquad \alpha < 1, c = 1, 2. \tag{1.1}$$

Here Y_{ij}^c and L_{ij}^c are output supply and labor input of firm j in country c. The index i means that the labor force of the firm belongs to union i. The productivity shocks have a common component across countries as well as country-specific components. Each firm in country c faces a demand for its output given by

$$D_{ij}^c = \left(\frac{P_{ij}}{P}\right)^{-\eta} H(r)G_c, \qquad \eta > 1, c = 1, 2, \tag{1.2}$$

where P_{ij} and P are the price charged by the individual firm and the general price level respectively, r is the real rate of interest, and η is the (absolute value of the) elasticity of demand facing the individual firm with respect to its relative price. The derivative of $H(r)$ with respect to r is negative, and G_c is a country-specific shock to the demands facing firms in country c. The logarithms of G_c have zero expected values. Equation (1.2) states that the demand facing the individual firm in country c is decreasing in the relative price of the product and in the real rate of interest. Demand shocks may have a common component across countries as well as country-specific components.

The general price level is defined as the integral, over the unit interval, of the (logaritms of) the prices of individual firms. It is convenient, for reasons that will become clearer later, to write this price level as

$$p = \frac{s_1}{n_1} \sum_{i=0}^{n_1-1} \left(\frac{\int_{\frac{i}{n_1}s_1}^{\frac{i+1}{n_1}s_1} p_{ij}^1 \, dj}{\int_{\frac{i}{n_1}s_1}^{\frac{i+1}{n_1}s_1} dj} \right) + \frac{s_2}{n_2} \sum_{i=0}^{n_2-1} \left(\frac{\int_{\frac{i}{n_2}s_2}^{\frac{i+1}{n_2}s_2} p_{ij}^2 \, dj}{\int_{\frac{i}{n_2}s_2}^{\frac{i+1}{n_2}s_2} dj} \right)$$

$$= \sum_{i=0}^{n_1-1} \int_{\frac{i}{n_1}s_1}^{\frac{i+1}{n_1}s_1} p_{ij}^1 \, dj + \sum_{i=0}^{n_2-1} \int_{\frac{i}{n_2}s_2}^{\frac{i+1}{n_2}s_2} p_{ij}^2 \, dj \equiv s_1 p_1 + s_2 p_2$$

$$= \int_0^1 p_{ij} \, dj, \tag{1.3}$$

where p_{ij}^c is the logarithm of P_{ij}^c, p is the logarithm of P, and p_c, $c = 1, 2$, is an index of the average level of the (logarithms of) prices of the products of country c.[3] This way of expressing the general price level facilitates the identification of the firms that are affected by an increase in the nominal wage rate set by union i. The general price level is a weighted average of the prices of goods produced in both countries. It represents the average price of the consumption basket of a typical individual. Since individuals in both countries consume all the goods produced in the MU, the summation of individual prices is over the entire unit interval, and the relevant general price index is the same for both countries.

The CB of the MU dislikes both inflation and unemployment. Its loss function is given by

$$\Gamma = u^2 + I\pi^2,   \tag{1.4}$$

where u and $\pi \equiv p - p_{-1}$ denote respectively the average rate of unemployment and price inflation in the MU. The parameter I is the (Rogoff 1985 type) degree of CB conservativeness, or weight-conservativeness.[4]

Nominal money demand in country c is given by

$$M_c^d = P K_c(i) Y_c^p,   \qquad c = 1, 2,   \tag{1.5}$$

where i is the nominal interest rate, Y_c^p is the permanent level of output in country c, and $K_c(i)$ is a (positively valued function) with a negative derivative.[5] Equilibrium in the union's money market implies that the sum of money demands over the two countries equals the total MU money supply M:

$$M = \left(K_1(i)Y_1^p + K_2(i)Y_2^p\right)P.$$

The monetary authority picks the total money supply in the union so as to achieve its desired value of the nominal rate, i. Solving for the nominal rate in terms of M, we have

$$i = F\left(\frac{M}{P}\right),   \tag{1.5a}$$

and the derivative of $F(M/P)$ with respect to M/P is negative.[6] Thus the choice of a given nominal rate is equivalent to the choice of a given level of real money balances. Hence the problem of the monetary authority can be viewed as a choice of the nominal money supply, taking into account the effect of this choice on the price level. The real rate of interest is defined as the nominal rate minus the expected rate of inflation, $r \equiv i - \pi^e$. We assume, for simplicity, that the choice of nominal rate by the monetary authority does not affect expected inflation so that any change in the nominal rate translates, one to one, into a change in the real rate. It follows from (1.2) and (1.5a) that

$$D_{ij}^c = \left(\frac{P_{ij}}{P}\right)^{-\eta} H\left\{F\left(\frac{M}{P}\right) - \pi^e\right\} G_c \equiv \left(\frac{P_{ij}}{P}\right)^{-\eta} h\left(\frac{M}{P}\right) G_c, \quad c = 1, 2,$$

where the constant value of π^e is subsumed into the functional form of $h(M/P)$. Since demand facing each firm is decreasing in the real rate, and since the real rate is decreasing in real money balances, $h(.)$ is an increasing function of real money balances. We assume for simplicity that $h(.)$ is the identity function so that demand facing an individual firm is[7]

$$D_{ij}^c = \left(\frac{P_{ij}}{P}\right)^{-\eta} \left(\frac{M}{P}\right) G_c, \qquad c = 1, 2. \tag{1.2a}$$

Each union desires a higher real wage and low unemployment of its members. We abstract from inflation-averse unions. The loss function of a typical union is:[8]

$$\Omega_i = -2w_{ri} + Au_i^2, \tag{1.6}$$

where w_{ri} is the (logarithm) of the real wage of union i's members, u_i is the rate of unemployment among them and A is a positive parameter that measures the relative importance attributed to employment versus the real wage by the union's leadership. This specification is in the spirit of labor union behavior theory as surveyed in Oswald (1982). Although the union cares about the real wage, it directly sets only the nominal wage. Prices and the money supply are more flexible than nominal wages, which are usually contractually fixed. Thus, in our model, wages are relatively sticky while product prices are fully flexible and—as in the classical tradition—respond to monetary policy shocks. This wage stickiness leaves some room for a stabilization policy by the CB.

We suppose that unions choose nominal wages prior to the realization of shocks, and that the Monetary Union's supply of money as well as individual prices in both countries are chosen after the realization of shocks. More precisely, we set up this model as a three-stage game. In the first stage every union in a country chooses its nominal wage so as to minimize the expected value of its loss function. In doing so, the union takes the nominal wages of other unions as given, forms forecasts of future productivity and demand shocks, and anticipates the reactions of the monetary authority and of firms to its nominal wage choice. The resulting nominal wages are then contractually fixed for the duration of the game. Essentially the union plays Nash against all other unions and acts as a Stackelberg leader with respect to the CB and the firms that are attached to it.

In the second stage of the game shocks occur, the monetary authority observes them, and chooses the nominal rate of interest in the MU so as to minimize the loss function. In doing so, it takes the preset nominal wages in both countries as given and anticipates the pricing reaction of firms to those wages, to the realizations of the shocks, and to its choice of instrument.

In the third and final stage every firm in the MU observes a nominal wage cost and the demand for its good. Taking those variables and the general price level as given, each firm sets its own price so as to maximize its real profits. The resulting string of first-order conditions, along with equation (1.3), simultaneously determines individual prices as well as the general price level. General equilibrium is characterized by solving the game using backward induction.

1.2.1 Price Setting

In the final stage, each firm observes the level of demand for its own product and sets a price that will maximize profits. By equations (1.1) and (1.2a), real profits of an individual firm in country c are given by

$$\Pi_{ij}^c = \frac{P_{ij}}{P} Y_{ij}^d - \frac{W_i}{P} L_{ij} = \left(\frac{P_{ij}}{P}\right)^{1-\eta} \frac{M}{P} G_c - \frac{W_i}{P} \left[\left(\frac{P_{ij}}{P}\right)^{-\eta} \frac{M}{P} \frac{G_c}{Z_c}\right]^{1/\alpha}.$$

$$(1.7)$$

As a firm chooses its own price, P_{ij}, it takes P, M, and the nominal wage, W_i, as given.[9] Maximizing profits with respect to P_{ij}, taking logarithms of both sides of the resulting expression, and rearranging, yields the following relative price level of firm j in country c:

$$p_{ij}^c - p = \theta + \frac{1}{\alpha + \eta(1 - \alpha)} \left[\alpha\left(w_i^c - p\right) + (1 - \alpha)(m - p + g_c) - z_c\right],$$

$$c = 1, 2. \quad (1.8)$$

Here $\theta \equiv [\alpha/(\alpha + \eta(1 - \alpha))] \log[\eta/\alpha(\eta - 1)]$, and the lowercase letters stand for the logarithms of the corresponding uppercase letters. In particular, $\log(Z_c) \equiv z_c$, where z_c is a random shock with $E(z_c) = 0$ and $E(z_c^2) = \sigma_{zc}^2$; similarly $\log(G_c) \equiv g_c$, where g_c is a random shock with $E(g_c) = 0$, $E(g_c^2) = \sigma_{gc}^2$, $c = 1, 2$. Equation (1.8) states that the optimal relative price of a typical monopolistically competitive firm is higher, (1) the higher is the real wage relative to the productivity shock, and (2) the higher real money balances in the MU. The first element reflects the firm's reaction to labor costs and the second its reaction to the demand for its product. The firm's derived demand for labor can be obtained by equating the product demand (equation 1.2a) with the firm's supply (equation 1.1). Taking logarithms of both sides of the resulting expression and rearranging results in

$$l_{ij}^{dc} = \frac{1}{\alpha}[-\eta(p_{ij} - p) + (m - p) + g_c - z_c], \qquad c = 1, 2. \tag{1.9}$$

Equation (1.9) states that the individual firm's derived demand for labor is an increasing function of real money balances and a decreasing function of its relative price. Equation (1.8) implies, in turn, that the relative price of the firm depends on the real wage it faces. Combined, the two equations imply that an increase in the real wage by a union reduces the demand for labor facing it.[10] This completes the analysis of firm j's optimal decision in the last stage of the game.

1.2.2 Choice of Money Supply (or Interest Rate) by the CB

In the second stage of the game the CB of the MU chooses the money supply after the realization of all shocks in the union. The CB sets the money supply so as to minimize its loss function in equation (1.4) taking the nominal wages set by labor unions as given, and anticipating the pricing and employment reaction of firms to its choice (as given by equations 1.8 and 1.9). The general price level in equation (1.3) can be rewritten as

$$p = s_1 p_1 + s_2 p_2, \tag{1.10}$$

where

$$p_1 \equiv \frac{\int_0^{s_1} p_{ij}^1 \, dj}{s_1} \quad \text{and} \quad p_2 \equiv \frac{\int_{s_1}^1 p_{ij}^2 \, dj}{s_2}. \tag{1.11}$$

The indexes p_1 and p_2 represent the average price levels of the goods produced by the firms in country 1 and country 2 respectively. Averaging equation (1.8) over firms within each country and rearranging, we obtain

$$s_2(p_1 - p_2) = \theta + \frac{1}{\alpha + \eta(1 - \alpha)}[\alpha(w_1 - p) + (1 - \alpha)(m - p + g_1) - z_1],$$

$$-s_1(p_1 - p_2) = \theta + \frac{1}{\alpha + \eta(1 - \alpha)}[\alpha(w_2 - p) + (1 - \alpha)(m - p + g_2) - z_2],$$

$$(1.12)$$

where w_c is the average nominal wage in country c.[11] Equations (1.10) through (1.12) determine the general price level, p, and its national components, p_1 and p_2 as functions of the shocks, the average nominal wages in the two countries, and the money supply of the MU. The solution that emerges for the rate of inflation is

$$\pi \equiv p - p_{-1} = [\alpha + \eta(1 - \alpha)]\theta + \alpha\bar{w} + (1 - \alpha)(m + \bar{g}) - \bar{z} - p_{-1},$$

$$(1.13)$$

where $\bar{w} \equiv s_1 w_1 + s_2 w_2$, $\bar{g} \equiv s_1 g_1 + s_2 g_2$, $\bar{z} \equiv s_1 z_1 + s_2 z_2$.

We now turn to a characterization of unemployment. Averaging equation (1.9) over firms within a given country yields the average level of demand for labor, and employment, per firm:

$$l_c^d = \frac{1}{\alpha}[-\eta(p_c - p) + (m - p) + g_c - z_c], \qquad c = 1, 2. \qquad (1.14)$$

Let $l_0 \equiv \log[L_0]$ be the logarithm of labor supply per firm. The average rate of unemployment per firm in country c coincides with the average country-specific rate of unemployment, which is given by

$$u_c = l_0 - l_c^d = l_0 + \frac{1}{\alpha}[\eta(p_c - p) - (m - p) + z_c - g_c], \qquad c = 1, 2.$$

$$(1.15)$$

Thus the rate of unemployment in country c is higher the higher are the average relative price of the products of that country, and the higher the country's productivity shock. Unemployment is lower, the higher the level of real money balances in the MU and the higher the demand shock for the products of the country. The positive relationship between productivity and unemployment reflects the fact that given the average relative price of the products of a country, the demand for labor of this country is lower when labor is more productive.[12] Let L_c and L_c^d

be total labor supply and total labor demand in country c. Unemployment in the monetary union is therefore

$$u = \frac{L_1 - L_1^d + L_2 - L_2^d}{L_1 + L_2}$$

$$= \frac{L_1}{L_1 + L_2} \frac{L_1 - L_1^d}{L_1} + \frac{L_2}{L_1 + L_2} \frac{L_2 - L_2^d}{L_2}$$

$$= s_1 u_1 + s_2 u_2. \tag{1.16}$$

Substituting equation (1.15) into equation (1.16), using equation (1.13) to substitute p out, and rearranging, we have

$$u = l_0 + \frac{\alpha + \eta(1 - \alpha)}{\alpha} \theta + \bar{w} - m - \bar{g}. \tag{1.17}$$

The fact that $\bar{z}$ does not affect aggregate unemployment might seem mysterious at first sight. The reason its impact is nil is that the direct (negative) effect of $\bar{z}$ on employment is exactly offset by the indirect general equilibrium effect of $\bar{z}$ on employment via real money balances. In particular, when $\bar{z}$ increases less labor is needed to produce a given level of output, so the demand for labor goes down. On the other hand, the increase in output reduces prices and raises real money balances. This stimulates demand for goods and, through it, the derived demand for labor. In the present model those two effects exactly offset each other making union wide unemployment independent of $\bar{z}$. By contrast, from equation (1.13), productivity shocks do have a first-order impact on inflation. As a consequence the motivation underlying the central bank's reaction to productivity shocks is solely to prevent fluctuations in the rate of inflation.[13]

Taking the average nominal wage in the MU as given, the CB chooses the nominal stock of money m so as to minimize its loss function. Substituting the expressions for inflation and unemployment (equations 1.13 and 1.17) into equation (1.4) and rearranging terms, the CB problem becomes

$$\min_{\{m\}} \left\{ \left[l_0 + \frac{\alpha + \eta(1 - \alpha)}{\alpha} \theta + \bar{w} - m - \bar{g} \right]^2 \right.$$

$$\left. + I[(\alpha + \eta(1 - \alpha))\theta + \alpha\bar{w} + (1 - \alpha)(m + \bar{g}) - \bar{z} - p_{-1}]^2 \right\}.$$

$$\tag{1.18}$$

This yields a reaction function for the CB in which the money supply is a linear function of the average nominal wage, $\bar{w}$, in the MU and of the average realizations of the productivity and demand shocks, $\bar{z}$ and $\bar{g}$:

$$m = \Psi + \frac{1 - \alpha(1 - \alpha)I}{1 + (1 - \alpha)^2 I}\bar{w} + \frac{(1 - \alpha)I}{1 + (1 - \alpha)^2 I}\bar{z} - \bar{g}, \tag{1.19}$$

where

$$\Psi \equiv \frac{l_0 + (1 - \alpha(1 - \alpha)I)\frac{\alpha + \eta(1 - \alpha)}{\alpha}\theta + (1 - \alpha)I p_{-1}}{1 + (1 - \alpha)^2 I}$$

is a constant. This reaction function has a number of notable features. First, the CB either counteracts or accommodates an increase in average, unionwide nominal wages depending on the degree of CB conservativeness (or independence), I. If the CB is sufficiently conservative, in the sense that $1 - \alpha(1 - \alpha)I < 0$, a wage increase triggers a tightening of the money supply. This extends the result found in the closed economy framework of CCD (2000) to the case of a MU composed of interdependent open economies. Evidence surveyed in CCD (2000) supports the view that, the highly conservative Bundesbank often tightened monetary policy in response to what it considered to be "excessive" wage settlements.[14] The discussion of the intuition underlying the response of the CB to the productivity and demand shocks is left to section 1.4 on stabilization policy.

1.2.3   Choice of Wages by Unions

In the first stage of the game, prior to the realization of shocks, each labor union takes nominal wages set by other unions in the MU as given and chooses its own nominal wage so as to minimize its *expected* losses from unemployment and a low real wage. Thus the typical labor union i minimizes $E(\Omega_i)$, where Ω_i is given by equation (1.6), and the expectation is taken over the distribution of shocks in the MU. In doing that, the labor union takes into consideration the consequences of its wage policy for the prices that will subsequently be set by firms, as well as the expected response of the CB in equation (1.19).

Let w_i and w_{-i} be respectively the nominal wage of labor union i and the average nominal wage of all other labor unions in the MU. Taking w_{-i} as given, labor union i sets a common wage, w_i, for all of its members, which are the workers attached to firms in the interval $[\frac{i}{n_c}s_c, \frac{i+1}{n_c}s_c]$, $c = 1, 2$. In the firms represented by labor union i, the relevant average rate of unemployment per firm is given by the difference between the number of workers attached to each firm and the average labor demand for a firm represented by labor union i:

$$u_i^c = l_0 - \left\{ \frac{\int_{\frac{i}{n_c} s_c}^{\frac{i+1}{n_c} s_c} l_{ij}^d \, dj}{\int_{\frac{i}{n_c} s_c}^{\frac{i+1}{n_c} s_c} dj} \right\} = l_0 - l_{ij}^{dc}, \qquad i \in c, c = 1, 2. \tag{1.20}$$

Since all firms in the interval $[\frac{i}{n_c} s_c, \frac{i+1}{n_c} s_c]$ face the same nominal wage w_i^c, equation (1.8) implies that $p_{ij}^c = p_i^c$ for all $j \in [\frac{i}{n_c} s_c, \frac{i+1}{n_c} s_c]$. Consequently labor union i anticipates that all the firms employing its members will react to the common wage level by setting the same relative price for their products. Thus equation (1.20) can be rewritten as

$$u_i^c = l_0 + \frac{1}{\alpha} \left[\eta \left(p_i^c - p \right) - (m - p) + z_c - g_c \right], \qquad i \in c, c = 1, 2. \tag{1.21}$$

Note that since all firms are identical, the unemployment *rate* among the members of labor union i's is also equal to u_i^c. By minimizing the union's expected loss function

$$E(\Omega_i) = E\left\{ -2\left(w_i^c - p \right) + A u_i^2 \right\}, \qquad i \in c, c = 1, 2 \tag{1.5a}$$

with respect to the nominal wage, w_i^c, we obtain the following family of first-order conditions:

$$E\left\{ -\left[1 - \frac{dp}{dw_i^c} \right] + A u_i^c \frac{du_i^c}{dw_i^c} \right\} = 0, \qquad i \in c, c = 1, 2. \tag{1.22}$$

Equation (1.22) illustrates the trade-offs facing a single labor union. The first term in equation (1.22) shows that when the union raises its nominal wage by one unit, the increase in its real wage is going to be somewhat smaller because the CB does not, generally, fully offset the inflationary consequences of wage push. Hence the effectiveness of an increase in the nominal wage in raising the real wage is less than full. On the other hand, the increase in the nominal wage raises the labor costs, and thus the *price* set by firms that use labor union i. This triggers two effects. An adverse competition effect and an aggregate demand effect, both of which are captured by the second term in equation (1.22).

First, the increase in prices makes firms whose workforce is controlled by union i less competitive, and thus it reduces their derived demands for labor. Second, the increase in prices generated by union i's wage push raises the *aggregate* price level. Consequently, for any given level of nominal money supply, real money balances shrink and aggregate demand falls across the entire MU. If a sufficiently conservative CB reacts to wage inflation by contracting the money supply, the aggregate demand will be depressed even further. As a result unemployment among union i workers will rise. Hence the optimization problem of the individual labor union involves balancing the benefit of a higher real wage against the cost of a higher rate of unemployment among its members.

Equation (1.22) provides a string of $n = n_1 + n_2$ equations from which the nominal wages of the n labor unions in the MU can be solved. We look for a symmetric equilibrium for nominal wages *within each country*, while allowing differences in nominal and in real wages across countries. The equilibrium outcomes are expressed in terms of the wage premium, defined as the expected difference between the actual and the competitive market-clearing wages. The equilibrium wage premium, ϕ_c, in country c, is

$$\phi_c = \frac{1}{A}\left\{(1-\alpha)q^c + \frac{\alpha s_{\bar{c}}}{\eta}(q^c - q^{\bar{c}})\right\}, \qquad c = 1, 2, \tag{1.23}$$

where the superscript $\bar{c}$ means "not c," and the explicit expression for q^c is

$$q^c = \frac{1 - \frac{s_c}{n_c}\left(\frac{1}{1+\alpha(1-\alpha)^2 I}\right)}{\frac{\eta}{\alpha+\eta(1-\alpha)}\left(1 - \frac{s_c}{n_c}\right) + \frac{s_c}{n_c}\frac{(1-\alpha)I}{1+\alpha(1-\alpha)^2 I}}, \qquad c = 1, 2. \tag{1.24}$$

A full derivation of the results is provided in the appendix at the end of this chapter. Note that the wage premia of the two countries differ if and only if $s_1/n_1 \neq s_2/n_2$. In particular, if $s_1/n_1 = s_2/n_2$, the expected wage premia are the same in both countries. Thus the differences in wage premia across countries reflect differences in country size and in the degree of CWB.

1.3   Roles of Country Size and of Wage Bargaining Institutions

The expected average wage premium in the MU is a fundamental determinant of inflation and of unemployment in the member countries. The expected average wage premium in the MU is defined as

$$\phi \equiv s_1\phi_1 + s_2\phi_2. \tag{1.25}$$

After substituting equation (1.23) into equation (1.25) and rearranging, we can express this expected value as

$$\phi = \frac{1-\alpha}{A}\{s_1 q^1 + s_2 q^2\}. \tag{1.26}$$

It is shown in the appendix that the expected value of average unemployment in the MU is

$$Eu \equiv E\left(s_1 u_1 + s_2 u_2\right) = \frac{1}{1-\alpha}\phi. \tag{1.27}$$

Thus the expected value of unemployment in the MU is proportional to the expected value of the average wage premium. We turn next to the determination of expected inflation. The first-order condition for the minimization problem of the monetary authority in equation (1.18) implies that

$$-u + I(1-\alpha)\pi = 0. \tag{1.28}$$

Applying the expected value operator to equation (1.28) and rearranging yields

$$E\pi = \frac{Eu}{I(1-\alpha)} = \frac{1}{I(1-\alpha)^2}\phi, \tag{1.29}$$

where the second equality follows from the extreme right-hand side of equation (1.27). Thus the rate of inflation in the MU is directly related to the wage premium.[15]

In what follows we analyze the effects of product market competitiveness, CB independence, and centralization in wage-setting on the equilibrium values of unemployment and inflation in the MU.

1.3.1   Effects of Competitiveness and of CB Conservativeness on MU-wide Variables

The larger the parameter η is in equation (1.2), the more substitutability there is among products and, therefore, the greater is the competition in the product markets within and among countries. The following proposition summarizes the effects of η on the MU-wide wage premium, unemployment, and inflation.[16]

Proposition 1.1   The more competitiveness there is in the product markets, as given by the parameter η, the lower are the expected average wage premium, the rate of unemployment, and the rate of inflation in the MU.

The intuition behind the proposition is straightforward. As product markets become more competitive the demand for labor of a typical labor union in the MU becomes more elastic and so the monopoly power of the individual labor union diminishes. As a consequence the wage premia and real wages are kept low, and unemployment is low as well. When there is low unemployment the Kydland-Prescott (1977) and Barro-Gordon (1983) (henceforth KPBG) inflation bias is low too, since the CB of the MU is less tempted to engage in expansionary monetary policy.

We turn next to an investigation of the effects of CB conservativeness on expected macroeconomic performance in the MU. The following proposition summarizes the main results.[17]

Proposition 1.2   The more conservative is the CB, the lower are the expected average wage premium, the average rate of unemployment, and the rate of inflation in the MU.

The intuition is again straightforward. A conservative CB is correctly expected to contract the money supply (or to expand it less) in response to inflationary union wage increases. This acts to deter the real wage demands of unions. Since, on average, when real wages are low, employment is high, the KPBG inflation bias is small. It is small both because of the direct effect of the money supply being constrained to thwart the expected inflation and because of the moderating effect the constrained supply of money has on the MU-wide expected wage premium, ϕ (see equation 1.29).[18]

Finally, we look at the effects of centralization in wage-setting on the expected macroeconomic performance in the MU:[19]

Proposition 1.3   The larger is the number of unions in the MU, the higher are the expected average wage premium, the average rate of unemployment, and the rate of inflation.

We now turn to a discussion of the proposition results. Clearly, a basic factor that checks the tendency of unions to raise real wages, and thus the wage premium, is the fear of unemployment among union members. This deterrent works via different channels. First, there is the relative price effect. An increase in the wage of a particular union raises the costs of firms that use its labor and so the affected firms will raise their prices. This depresses sales, and thus the demand for the union's workforce.

Two additional mechanisms will increase unemployment not only among the members of the union considered, but also among the members of other unions. One is related to the fact that an increase in the nominal wage of the single union raises the general price level. Then, in the absence of a policy response, the higher price level will depress real money balances and aggregate demand for goods and thus for labor as well. The other is related to the expected response of the CB. A relatively liberal CB (I is low) will counteract much of the contractionary economywide effects of the increase in the union's nominal wage by increasing the nominal money supply (equivalently, by reducing the interest rate). A conservative CB (I is high) will respond by reducing the nominal money supply, which further reduces real balances and the demands for goods and labor.[20] However, even when the CB is relatively liberal, the increase in a single union's wages will have a negative combined effect on the aggregate labor demand.

We turn now to a discussion of proposition 1.3. When the number of labor unions is small, the individual union is large. A large union can better internalize adverse aggregate consequences of its wage demands for employment. Unions' fear of unemployment becomes weaker the larger the number of unions in the MU.[21] The macroeconomic effects described by proposition 1.3 can be calculated in terms of the expected value of real money balances in the MU. We can thus show that

$$E(m - p) = -\frac{[\alpha + \eta(1 - \alpha)]\theta}{1 - \alpha} - \frac{\alpha}{1 - \alpha}(\phi + Ew_{rc}), \qquad (1.30)$$

where Ew_{rc} denotes the expected value of the competitive wage.[22] Equation (1.30) implies that the average level of real money balances in the MU is inversely related to the real wage premium. The intuition underlying proposition 1.3 can now be stated as follows: as the number of unions increases, so do the real wage premium and the rate of unemployment, but real money balances and the aggregate demand for labor decrease. With high unemployment, the incentive of the CB would be to expand the money supply. As a result the KPBG inflation bias will rise.

1.3.2 Determinants of Country-Specific Average Performance

The following proposition summarizes the effects of country size and of country specific CWB for the expected values of country specific variables.[23]

Proposition 1.4

i. The country with a higher ratio, s_c/n_c, has a lower expected wage premium and a lower expected rate of unemployment.

ii. Where two countries are of the same size, the country with the more decentralized wage-bargaining system (more unions) has a higher expected real wage premium and a higher expected rate of unemployment.

iii. Where two countries have the same degrees of centralization in wage bargaining ($n_1 = n_2$), the smaller country has a higher expected real wage premium and a higher expected rate of unemployment.

Part ii of the proposition is supported by empirical evidence presented by Nickell (1997, 1999) and OECD (1997).

Before turning to a discussion of the intuition behind the country-specific results, it will be useful to derive an expression for the level of relative competitiveness between the two countries. It is shown in section 1.6.7 of the appendix that the relative price of the products produced in country c is

$$p_c - p = \frac{s_{\bar{c}}}{\alpha + \eta(1-\alpha)} \{\alpha(w_c - w_{\bar{c}}) + (1-\alpha)(g_c - g_{\bar{c}}) - (z_c - z_{\bar{c}})\},$$

$$c = 1, 2. \quad (1.31)$$

The expected value of this expression is

$$E(p_c - p) = \frac{s_{\bar{c}}}{\alpha + \eta(1-\alpha)} \alpha E(w_c - w_{\bar{c}})$$

$$= \frac{s_{\bar{c}}}{\alpha + \eta(1-\alpha)} \alpha(\phi_c - \phi_{\bar{c}}), \qquad c = 1, 2, \quad (1.32)$$

where the second equality is a direct consequence of equation (A1.14) in the appendix. Equation (1.32) shows that the country with a higher wage premium charges a higher price for its products and is therefore less competitive than the country with the lower wage premium. This observation, in conjunction with the fact that q^c is decreasing in s_c and increasing in n_c (see the proof of proposition 1.3 in the appendix) yields the following:

Proposition 1.5

i. If the two countries are of equal size, the country with more decentralized bargaining in the labor market is, on average, less competitive.

ii. Where two countries have similar CWBs, the smaller country is, on average, less competitive.

iii. More generally, country 1 is more or less competitive than country 2 depending on whether s_1/n_1 is larger or smaller than s_2/n_2.

Propositions 1.4 and 1.5 imply that despite the common monetary policy, real wages, unemployment, and competitiveness differ across the two countries in the MU even in the absence of shocks. The intuition underlying these results is related to the preceding discussion. In particular, the larger the number of unions in a country and the smaller the country's size, the smaller will be the extent to which a representative union in that country will internalize the adverse macroeconomic consequences of its wage decisions for employment. As a consequence the real wage premium will be higher. Finally, a country with higher real wages will be less competitive in its trade with the other country as noted in proposition 1.5 and illustrated by the extreme right-hand side of equation (1.32).

The following proposition summarizes the effect of CBC, I, on the expected rates of unemployment within each country.[24]

Proposition 1.6 Other things the same, the more conservative the CB, the lower will be the expected unemployment rate in each country of the MU.

1.4   Stabilization Policy

The CB of the MU dislikes variability in both inflation and employment. But, since it has only one instrument, in general, the CB cannot fully offset the effect of shocks. It therefore compromises by choosing the money supply (or the interest rate) so as to equate the marginal cost of inflation variability to the marginal cost of MU-wide employment variability. But, as can be seen from equation (1.19), it is nonetheless optimal for the CB to fully offset the effect of the unionwide average demand shock on the demand for goods in the MU. The reason is that aggregate demand shocks do not require the CB to compromise between reducing inflation variability and employment variability. By fully offseting the velocity effects and other demand shocks on the economy, the CB can reduce fluctuations in both inflation and unemployment. This intuition is similar to that found in new Keynesian models of monetary policy of the type reviewed by Clarida, Gali, and Gertler (1999). But in the MU this implies that demand shocks facing producers in a country cannot be fully offset unless the demand shocks are perfectly correlated across countries.

Equation (1.19) implies that the CB accommodates the MU-wide average productivity shock, $\bar{z}$. The reason is that the unionwide average productivity shock does not directly affect unemployment but it does affect inflation. For this reason the CB's monetary policy is to offset the effects of fluctuations in productivity only on inflation.[25] This way in the face of a positive (negative) productivity shock the money supply is increased (reduced).

Interestingly a more independent CB (in terms of high I) would be more reactive. The reasoning is that a CB that is relatively more averse to inflation fluctuations would find it advantageous to be more reactive in order to offset a larger fraction of the effects of productivity shocks on the inflation.[26] Recent evidence for Germany provided by Berger and Woitek (1999) is consistent with this intuition. Berger and Woitek found that when the Bundesbank Council was controlled by a more conservative group, the monetary policy responded more strongly to exogenous shocks.

1.4.1 Effects of a Common Stabilization Policy on MU-wide Unemployment and Inflation

To evaluate the effects of shocks on inflation in the presence of a common stabilization policy, we substitute equation (1.19) into equation (1.13) and rearrange it to yield

$$\pi = \frac{1}{1 + (1-\alpha)^2 I} \left\{ (1-\alpha)l_0 + \frac{[\alpha + \eta(1-\alpha)]\theta}{\alpha} + \bar{w} - p_{-1} - \bar{z} \right\}. \quad (1.33)$$

Note that the MU-wide aggregate demand shock does not appear in this expression. This confirms that independently of its level of conservativeness, the CB always fully offsets the effect of the aggregate demand shock on MU-wide inflation. But the CB allows some of the MU-wide aggregate supply shock, $\bar{z}$, to affect the rate of inflation. Thus

a negative, unionwide, supply shock is partially allowed to raise inflation and inflation variability. Only in the limit, where the CB is extremely conservative (I tends to ∞), inflation and its variability become
independent of productivity shocks.

We turn next to the MU-wide rate of unemployment. The MU-wide
rate of unemployment is[27]

$$u = \frac{1}{1-\alpha}\left\{\phi - \frac{(1-\alpha)^2 I}{1+(1-\alpha)^2 I}\bar{z}\right\}. \tag{1.34}$$

Again, this expression shows that the effect of the aggregate demand
shock on unemployment is fully offset, although productivity shocks
partially affect the MU-wide rate of unemployment. The more liberal
the CB (the lower I) the smaller will be the fraction of the MU-wide
average productivity shock that is allowed to affect the unemployment
rate. In the limit where the CB becomes ultraliberal (I tends to 0), the
effect of $\bar{z}$ on MU unemployment is fully neutralized.[28] As can be seen
from equation (1.33), in this case, supply shocks are fully passed on
to inflation.

1.4.2   Country-Specific Effects of Shocks under a Common Stabilization Policy

Since the policy of the CB of the MU is geared to the stabilization of a
weighted average of the shocks in the monetary union, the country-
specific shocks are obviously not stabilized to the same extent that they
would have been under national monetary policies. The remainder of
this section focuses on the differential effects of the common stabilization policy in the face of heterogeneous cross country shocks.

Effects on Relative Competitiveness within the MU

Not surprisingly, equation (1.31) suggests that the level of competitiveness of a country in the MU, as measured by the average relative price
of the products of that country, depends on the differences between the
demand and productivity shocks of the two countries. Other things
the same, the country with a relatively high productivity shock enjoys
more competitiveness (a lower relative price) while the producers in
that country set relatively high prices on experiencing a relatively high
demand shock. Finally, the impact of the productivity and demand
shocks is lower when the elasticity of substitution among products, η,
is high.

Effects of Shocks on Country-Specific Rates of Unemployment

It is shown in section 1.6 of the appendix that

$$u_c = \frac{\phi_c}{1-\alpha} + \frac{\alpha s_{\bar{c}}}{(1-\alpha)(\alpha+\eta(1-\alpha))} (\phi_{\bar{c}} - \phi_c)$$

$$- \frac{(1-\alpha)I(\alpha+\eta(1-\alpha)-s_{\bar{c}})+s_{\bar{c}}(\eta-1)}{[\alpha+\eta(1-\alpha)](1+(1-\alpha)^2I)} z_c$$

$$- \frac{s_{\bar{c}}((1-\alpha)I-(\eta-1))}{[\alpha+\eta(1-\alpha)](1+(1-\alpha)^2I)} z_{\bar{c}} + \frac{s_{\bar{c}}}{\alpha+\eta(1-\alpha)}(g_{\bar{c}} - g_c), \qquad (1.35)$$

where $c = 1, 2$. A close look at this expression reveals some interesting interactions. First, despite the fact that the CB fully offsets the MU-wide average demand shock, $\bar{g}$, the difference between the demand shocks that hit the two countries **does** affect the country-specific rates of unemployment. In particular, when the two demand shocks are not perfectly correlated, the domestic rate of unemployment is higher when the demand shock in the other country is larger than the one in the domestic economy. The reason is that the monetary authority responds to a positive, MU-wide demand shock by reducing the money supply. When the demand shock in the other country is larger, the CB contracts more than what is needed to stabilize the domestic economy, creating a high rate of unemployment. This negative externality is more important when the country is relatively small, and less important when product markets are relatively competitive (η is high). Note that the magnitude of this cross effect is independent of central bank conservativeness. This is due to the fact that all central bankers tend to stabilize the MU-wide average demand shock in the same way.

The own productivity shock affects domestic unemployment via three channels that can be seen more explicitly by referring to equation (1.15). An increase in domestic productivity directly raises domestic unemployment since less labor is needed to satisfy the demand for the country's products. On the other hand, an increase in domestic productivity also raises the country's competitiveness and real money balances in the MU. These two effects raise the demand for domestic products and reduce domestic unemployment. Equation (1.35) shows that the last two (indirect) effects dominate the first (direct) effect. Note that the absolute value of the marginal impact of a domestic productivity shock on domestic unemployment is larger when the central bank is more conservative (I is large). A more conservative CB accommodates productivity shocks through stronger adjustments of real money balances.

In raising real money balances, an increase in foreign productivity reduces domestic unemployment. On the other hand, an increase in foreign productivity also reduces the competitiveness of domestically produced products, thereby raising domestic unemployment. When the CB of the MU is sufficiently conservative, the first effect dominates and an increase in foreign productivity reduces domestic unemployment. More precisely, the coefficient attached to the foreign productivity shock in equation (1.35) implies the following:

Proposition 1.7   An increase in foreign productivity reduces domestic unemployment if and only if

$$I > \frac{\eta - 1}{1 - \alpha}. \tag{1.36}$$

Relative Variability of National Rates of Unemployment in a MU
Equation (1.35) provides the ingredients needed to identify some of the factors that affect the relative size of the variances of national rates of unemployment in a MU. It is instructive to look at two extreme cases. In the first case, the variability of unemployment is driven only by demand shocks. In the second case, the unemployment variability is driven only by supply shocks.

Role of Demand Shocks   When the variance of productivity shocks is zero, equation (1.35) implies that

$$\text{var}(u_1) - \text{var}(u_2) = K_D \cdot [s_2 - s_1] = K_D \cdot [1 - 2s_1], \tag{1.37}$$

where $K_D \equiv E[g_2 - g_1]^2/[\alpha + \eta(1 - \alpha)] > 0$. This implies that the smaller country experiences wider, demand-induced, fluctuations in unemployment. This is because the CB of the MU stabilizes mainly the demand shock of the large country. As a consequence the small country will experience large shifts in demand that are entirely induced by the CB stabilization policy.

Role of Productivity Shocks   Assume that the variance of demand shocks is zero, and for simplicity, consider the case where $\text{var}(z_1) = \text{var}(z_2)$. Let $\rho \equiv \text{cov}(z_1, z_2)/\sqrt{\text{var}(z_1) \cdot \text{var}(z_2)} \in [-1, 1]$ be the correlation coefficient between the productivity shocks in the two countries. It follows that

$$\text{var}(u_1) - \text{var}(u_2) = -K_S \cdot [(1-\alpha)I - (\eta-1)] \cdot (1-\rho) \cdot [s_2 - s_1], \qquad (1.38)$$

where K_s is a positive constant. This expression implies that the variability of unemployment is the same when the countries are of equal size (i.e., $s_1 = s_2$), or if their productivity shocks are perfectly and positively correlated (i.e., $\rho = 1$). The relation between country size and relative variability in unemployment crucially depends on the sign of $[(1-\alpha)I - (\eta-1)]$, which is positive if inequality (1.36) holds. In this case the variance of unemployment in the larger country is higher. The result depends on the fact that when it is sufficiently conservative, the CB does not care much about variability in employment. However, whichever its type, the CB responds more to the productivity shocks of the larger country (because those shocks have a stronger impact on inflation within the Monetary Union). A positive shock in the large country will reduce unemployment both by increasing its competitiveness and by triggering an accommodating money supply; see equation (1.19). For the smaller country, the worsening in competitiveness is compensated by the increase in money supply, thus reducing the effect of the foreign shock on unemployment.

1.5   Concluding Remarks

Rather than summarize the results of the chapter, we will briefly consider the implications of our framework for issues like the possible effects of the creation of the ECB on macroeconomic performance in the euro area, the incentives for labor market reform and the optimal level of central bank conservativeness in a MU.

As was shown by Cukierman and Lippi (2001), the creation of a MU tends to raise real wages by reducing the relative size of a typical union involved in strategic interactions with the CB. This adverse strategic effect raises both inflation and unemployment.[29] However, Gasiorek (2000) claimed that the creation of the euro, increases the transparency of relative prices across countries within the EMU and thus creates more competition in the product markets. The results of this chapter indicate that an increase in the level of competition in the product markets reduces real wages in the Monetary Union, and consequently inflation and unemployment. To the extent that the creation of the EMU will raise competition in the goods markets the adverse strategic effect may be offset.

The creation of the EMU, however, did not leave the average level of central bank conservativeness in the euro area unaltered. For many countries in the euro domain, the creation of the ECB has raised the level of CB conservativeness. The results of this chapter show that such an institutional change would reduce the real wage demands of unions and along with that, unemployment and the inflation bias. Although a highly conservative ECB may result in insufficient stabilizations of fluctuations in employment, our results unambiguously establish that expected average performance with respect to both inflation and unemployment is better under the more conservative CB.[30] We have, indeed, the familiar Rogoff (1985) generalized trade-off between better average performance in inflation (and, here, in unemployment) and stabilization policy.[31]

Recent work has looked at the effects of monetary integration on the incentives for labor market reform (Calmfors 1998, 2001a, b; Sibert 2000). In particular, Sibert and Sutherland (2000) find that the incentive for labor market reforms that increase wage flexibility to shocks may or may not be stronger under a MU than under national monetary policies. This chapter does not provide a explicit answer to this question. But it suggests that by devoting less attention to employment stabilization, a relatively conservative ECB could stimulate labor market reform in a direction that would make real wages more responsive to the macroeconomic effects of supply shocks. One way to achieve lower real wage rigidity is by enhanced coordination of labor unions within the EMU. More precisely, in our model this requires an effective reduction in the number of unions. Coordination among unions may even arise spontaneously as in Holden (2001), or through some centralized initiative on the part of governments as was the case with income policies during the 1970s (Flanagan, Soskice, and Ulman 1983). In the context of the EMU such initiative would require the participation of individual governments or intervention from European community institutions.

We end with two more general remarks on the timing of events postulated in this chapter and on the transmission mechanism of monetary policy featured in it. Obviously, under a different timing some of the theoretical results may change. But we believe that the timing postulated here captures the most important dynamic, real life components of the interactions among firms, the central bank, and labor unions without the burden of a fully blown dynamic model. The timing of events we selected reflects the fact that pricing in the economy is adjusted more frequently than monetary policy, and that monetary policy, in turn, is adjusted more frequently than contractually fixed nominal wages. Casual observation suggests that other possible timing assumptions, such as when firms commit to prices before the central bank sets the interest rate or the money supply, appear to be relatively counterfactual, at least under discretionary monetary policy.

Recently revived, the new Keynesian models anchor much of the real effects of monetary policy on sticky prices and aggregate demand management, rather than on a Friedman-Lucas expectations augmented Phillips relation in which the transmission of monetary policy operates via aggregate supply.[32] Our framework postulates that nominal wages are contractually fixed for some time but allows for full price flexibility. An advantage of our framework is that it captures the effects of monetary policy on economic activity through both the aggregate demand and the aggregate supply channels. The first channel operates through the effect that monetary expansion has on the demand for goods, and through it on the derived demand for labor and employment. The supply channel of the transmission process also operates in the model since the CB can react to shocks that had not been anticipated at the time wage contracts were concluded. As a consequence the CB has some capacity to stabilize the level of employment also by lowering or raising the *ex post* real wage through the creation of inflation that had not been anticipated at the time nominal wage contracts were signed.

1.6   Appendix

1.6.1   Derivation of Equilibrium Wage Premia

A first step toward the solution of the n-equations system in (1.22) involves the characterization of the effects of an increase in the nominal wage w_i^c of the union on the general price level p and on the rate of unemployment u_i^c among the members of union i. Eliminating p_{-1} on both sides of equation (1.13) and differentiating the resulting expression with respect to w_i^c, we have

$$\frac{dp}{dw_i^c} = \alpha \frac{s_c}{n_c} + (1 - \alpha)\frac{dm}{dw_i^c}, \qquad i \in c, c = 1, 2. \tag{A1.1}$$

To find the impact of an increase in the union's nominal wage rate on the choice of money supply by the CB of the MU, we differentiate equation (1.19) with respect to w_i^c. Substituting the resulting expression into equation (A1.1) and rearranging, we have

$$\frac{dp}{dw_i^c} = \frac{s_c}{n_c}\left(\frac{1}{1+\alpha(1-\alpha)^2 I}\right), \qquad i \in c, c = 1, 2. \tag{A1.2}$$

Note that this expression is smaller than 1 and is increasing in country size and decreasing in the number of unions in that country. The intuition is obvious. Since the CB of the MU responds to MU-wide aggregates, the effect of the nominal wage decisions of a particular union in a country on the reaction of the CB is smaller the smaller the country of that union, and the larger the number of unions in it. We turn next to a calculation of the impact of the union's wage choice on unemployment among its members. Differentiating equation (1.21) with respect to w_i^c yields

$$\frac{du_i^c}{dw_i^c} = \frac{1}{\alpha}\left[\eta\frac{d(p_i^c - p)}{dw_i^c} - \frac{d(m - p)}{dw_i^c}\right], \qquad i \in c, c = 1, 2. \tag{A1.3}$$

The expression for $(m - p)$ can be obtained as follows: Multiplying the first equation in (1.12) by s_1, the second one by s_2, and substracting the second equation from the first one, we obtain

$$0 = \theta + \frac{1}{\alpha + \eta(1-\alpha)}\left[\alpha(\bar{w} - p) + (1-\alpha)(m - p + \bar{g}) - \bar{z}\right]. \tag{A1.4}$$

Thus real money balances in the MU are given by

$$m - p = -\frac{[\alpha + \eta(1-\alpha)]\theta}{1-\alpha} - \frac{\alpha}{1-\alpha}(\bar{w} - p) - \bar{g} + \frac{\bar{z}}{1-\alpha}. \tag{A1.5}$$

Differentiating equation (A1.5) with respect to w_i^c, using equation (A1.2), and rearranging, we obtain

$$\frac{d(m - p)}{dw_i^c} = -\frac{s_c}{n_c}\left(\frac{\alpha(1-\alpha)I}{1+\alpha(1-\alpha)^2 I}\right), \qquad i \in c, c = 1, 2. \tag{A1.6}$$

Thus an increase in the nominal wage of union i induces a decrease in aggregate real money balances in the MU. This is due to the fact that although the CB of the MU allows some of the inflationary impact of the wage increase to be passed on in the form of higher prices, it does not fully compensate for the consequent reduction in real money balances. As a consequence aggregate real money balances go down. Not surprisingly, this effect is smaller, the smaller the country of the labor union in question and the larger the number of unions in this country. Note also that the higher the level of CB conservativeness, I, the larger the consequent reduction in real money balances.

Differentiating equation (1.8) with respect to w_i^c, and recalling that all the firms using the labor of union i set the same price, we obtain

$$\frac{d\left(p_i^c - p\right)}{dw_i^c} = \frac{1}{\alpha + \eta(1 - \alpha)}\left[\alpha\left(1 - \frac{dp}{dw_i^c}\right) + (1 - \alpha)\frac{d(m - p)}{dw_i^c}\right],$$

$$i \in c, c = 1, 2. \quad (A1.7)$$

Substituting equations (A1.6) and (A1.7) into equation (A1.3) and rearranging yields

$$\frac{du_i^c}{dw_i^c} = \frac{\eta}{\alpha + \eta(1 - \alpha)}\left(1 - \frac{s_c}{n_c}\right) + \frac{s_c}{n_c}\frac{(1 - \alpha)I}{1 + \alpha(1 - \alpha)^2 I} \equiv Q_u^c,$$

$$i \in c, c = 1, 2. \quad (A1.8)$$

Equation (A1.8) shows that the marginal impact of an increase in the nominal wage of a union on the rate of unemployment among its members is positive and is the same for all unions within a given country. Furthermore it does not depend on the realizations of shocks in the MU, and it is uniformly larger the higher the degree of competitiveness on product markets (the higher η), and the higher the level of CB conservativeness. From equation (A1.2) the marginal impact of an increase in the nominal wage of the union on its real wage is

$$1 - \frac{dp}{dw_i^c} = 1 - \frac{s_c}{n_c}\left(\frac{1}{1 + \alpha(1 - \alpha)^2 I}\right) \equiv Q_w^c, \quad i \in c, c = 1, 2. \quad (A1.9)$$

Equation (A1.9) is the elasticity of the real wage of a union with respect to the union's nominal wage. Expression (A1.9) implies that this elasticity is bounded between 0 and 1. Furthermore, it is larger the larger CB conservativeness, I, the smaller the relative size of the country of the union under consideration, and the larger the number of unions in that country. Since the marginal impacts of w_i^c on the real wage of a union and on its unemployment do not depend on the realizations of shocks in the MU,

$$E\left[1 - \frac{dp}{dw_i^c}\right] = 1 - \frac{dp}{dw_i^c}, \quad E\left[\frac{du_i^c}{dw_i^c}\right] = \frac{du_i^c}{dw_i^c}, \quad i \in c, c = 1, 2. \quad (A1.10)$$

Combining equation (A1.10) and equation (1.22) results in

$$-Q_w^c + AQ_u^c Eu_i^c \equiv -\left[1 - \frac{dp}{dw_i^c}\right] + A\frac{du_i^c}{dw_i^c}Eu_i^c = 0, \qquad i \in c, c = 1, 2.$$

(A1.11)

We now determine the expressions for Eu_i^c. In applying the expected value operator to equation (1.21) and exploiting expressions (1.8) and (A1.5), we see that in a symmetric equilibrium within each country,

$$Eu^1 = l_0 + \frac{((1-\alpha)\eta + \alpha)\theta}{\alpha(1-\alpha)} + \frac{((1-\alpha)\eta + \alpha s_1)Ew_r^1 + \alpha s_2 Ew_r^2}{(1-\alpha)(\alpha + (1-\alpha)\eta)},$$

$$Eu^2 = l_0 + \frac{((1-\alpha)\eta + \alpha)\theta}{\alpha(1-\alpha)} + \frac{((1-\alpha)\eta + \alpha s_2)Ew_r^2 + \alpha s_1 Ew_r^1}{(1-\alpha)(\alpha + (1-\alpha)\eta)},$$

(A1.12)

where Ew_r^c is the expected value, prior to the realization of shocks in the MU, of the real wage in country c.

It is convenient to find the (expected value of the) competitive real wage in each country. The system of equations in (A1.12) yields the competitive real wages in the two countries when the expected excess supply of labor in each country is zero. Setting $Eu^1 = Eu^2 = 0$ in (A1.12) and rearranging yields

$$\frac{((1-\alpha)\eta + \alpha s_1)Ew_{rc}^1 + \alpha s_2 Ew_{rc}^2}{(1-\alpha)(\alpha + (1-\alpha)\eta)} = -\left\{l_0 + \frac{((1-\alpha)\eta + \alpha)\theta}{\alpha(1-\alpha)}\right\},$$

$$\frac{\alpha s_1 Ew_{rc}^1 + ((1-\alpha)\eta + \alpha s_2)Ew_{rc}^2}{(1-\alpha)(\alpha + (1-\alpha)\eta)} = -\left\{l_0 + \frac{((1-\alpha)\eta + \alpha)\theta}{\alpha(1-\alpha)}\right\},$$

(A1.13)

where Ew_{rc}^1 and Ew_{rc}^2 are the expected values of the competitive real wages in the two countries. Due to the symmetry of the system in (A1.13) the competitive real wages in the two countries are identical. The common solution is given by

$$Ew_{rc}^1 = Ew_{rc}^2 = -\left\{(1-\alpha)l_0 + ((1-\alpha)\eta + \alpha)\frac{\theta}{\alpha}\right\} \equiv Ew_{rc}.$$
(A1.14)

We now come to the final step of the solution. Substituting equation (A1.12) into the first-order condition in equation (A1.11) (for $c = 1$ and for $c = 2$) and using the solution for the competitive real wage in

(A1.14) yields, after some rearrangement,

$$((1-\alpha)\eta + \alpha s_1)\phi_1 + \alpha s_2 \phi_2 = \frac{(1-\alpha)(\alpha + (1-\alpha)\eta)}{A} \frac{Q_w^1}{Q_u^1},$$

$$\alpha s_1 \phi_1 + ((1-\alpha)\eta + \alpha s_2)\phi_2 = \frac{(1-\alpha)(\alpha + (1-\alpha)\eta)}{A} \frac{Q_w^2}{Q_u^2}, \tag{A1.15}$$

where

$$\phi_c \equiv E\left(w_r^c - w_{rc}\right) = E w_r^c - E w_{rc}, \qquad c = 1, 2, \tag{A1.16}$$

is the (expected value of the) difference between the equilibrium wage in country c and the competitive real wage rate. Following CCD (2000), we refer to ϕ_c as the "wage premium" in country c. Equations (A1.15) are the (implicit) reaction functions of the two countries to each other (expected values of) real wages. They imply that the real wages in the two countries are strategic substitutes. When the real wage in one country is higher, the real wage chosen by the other country is lower. The reason is that a higher real wage in, say, country 2 leads to a higher general price level and depresses real money balances in the MU (see equation A1.5). As a consequence the level of demand facing firms in country 1 is lower and so are their derived demands for labor. Labor unions in country 1 must content themselves with lower expected real wages. Equations (A1.15) provide a system of two simultaneous equations that determines the wage premia in the two countries. The solutions are given by

$$\phi_c = \frac{1}{A} \left\{ (1-\alpha)\frac{Q_w^c}{Q_u^c} + \frac{\alpha s_{\bar{c}}}{\eta}\left(\frac{Q_w^c}{Q_u^c} - \frac{Q_w^{\bar{c}}}{Q_u^{\bar{c}}}\right) \right\}, \qquad c = 1, 2, \tag{A1.17}$$

where the superscript $\bar{c}$ means "not c." For example, if $c = 1$, $\bar{c} = 2$. We denote $q^c \equiv Q_w^c / Q_u^c$. The explicit expression for q^c is reported in expression (1.24) in the text.

1.6.2 Derivation of Equation (1.27)

From the expression for the competitive real wage (equation A1.14), it is possible to rewrite equations (A1.12) as

$$Eu^1 = \frac{((1-\alpha)\eta + \alpha s_1)\phi_1 + \alpha s_2 \phi_2}{(1-\alpha)(\alpha + (1-\alpha)\eta)},$$

$$Eu^2 = +\frac{((1-\alpha)\eta + \alpha s_2)\phi_2 + \alpha s_1 \phi_1}{(1-\alpha)(\alpha + (1-\alpha)\eta)}. \tag{A1.18}$$

Since $s_1 + s_2 = 1$, these equations can be rewritten, after some algebra, as

$$Eu^1 = \frac{\phi_1}{(1-\alpha)} + \frac{\alpha s_2(\phi_2 - \phi_1)}{(1-\alpha)(\alpha + (1-\alpha)\eta)},$$

$$\quad \text{(A1.19)}$$

$$Eu^2 = \frac{\phi_2}{(1-\alpha)} - \frac{\alpha s_1(\phi_2 - \phi_1)}{(1-\alpha)(\alpha + (1-\alpha)\eta)}.$$

The extreme right-hand side of equation (1.27) is obtained by substituting the last two equations into the middle part of (1.27) and by rearranging.

1.6.3 Proof of Proposition 1.1
Examination of equation (1.24) reveals that q^c is a decreasing function of η. It follows, from equations (1.26), (1.27), and (1.29) that the MU-wide expected values of the wage premium, the rate of unemployment, and inflation are all decreasing in η.

1.6.4 Proof of Proposition 1.2
Differentiating equation (1.24) with respect to I and rearranging gives

$$\frac{\partial q^c}{\partial I} = -\frac{(1-\alpha)\left\{2(1-\alpha)^2 I + 1 - \frac{s_c}{n_c}\right\}\frac{s_c}{n_c}}{\left[\frac{\eta(1+\alpha(1-\alpha)^2 I)}{\alpha + \eta(1-\alpha)}\left(1 - \frac{s_c}{n_c}\right) + (1-\alpha)I\frac{s_c}{n_c}\right]^2} < 0.$$

Application of this result to equation (1.26) implies that the expected, MU-wide, wage premium is lower, the higher is I. It then follows immediately from equations (1.27) and (1.29) that the expected values of unemployment and of inflation in the MU are lower the higher the I.

1.6.5 Proof of Proposition 1.3
We first show that q^c is a decreasing function of s_c and an increasing function of n_c. Let $\tau_c \equiv s_c/n_c$. Differentiating q^c with respect to τ_c yields

$$\frac{\partial q^c}{\partial \tau_c} = \frac{-\alpha(1-\alpha)I}{\left(Q_u^c\right)^2(\alpha + \eta(1-\alpha))(1 + \alpha(1-\alpha)^2 I)} < 0, \quad c = 1, 2.$$

Proposition 1.3 follows from equations (1.26), (1.27), and (1.29), together with the fact that q^c is increasing in n_c.

1.6.6 Proof of Proposition 1.4
The proof of part i is obtained by substituting equation (1.23) into equations (A1.18). After some algebra this yields

$$Eu^c = \frac{q^c}{A}, \qquad c = 1, 2.$$

The proof of part i is completed by using the fact that $\partial q^c / \partial \tau_c < 0$. Parts ii and iii are particular cases of part i.

1.6.7 Derivation of Equation (1.31)

Expressions (1.12) provide a system of two simulataneous equations from which the average price levels of the goods produced in the two countries (p_1 and p_2) can be solved in terms of the nominal wages, the money supply, and the realized shocks. The solutions are given by

$$p_c = \theta D + \frac{1}{D}\{(s_{\bar{c}} + Ds_c)[\alpha w_c + (1-\alpha)(m + g_c) - z_c]$$
$$+ s_{\bar{c}}(D-1)[\alpha w_{\bar{c}} + (1-\alpha)(m + g_{\bar{c}}) - z_{\bar{c}}]\}, \qquad c = 1, 2.$$

(A1.20)

where $D \equiv \alpha + \eta(1-\alpha)$. Equation (1.31) is obtained by substracting p, obtained from equation (1.13), from equation (A1.20) and by rearranging.

1.6.8 Derivation of Equation (1.35)

Substituting equation (1.31) for the relative price in country c ($c = 1, 2$) into the expression for u_c (equation 1.15) and rearranging

$$u_c = \frac{-Ew_{rc}}{(1-\alpha)}$$

$$+ \frac{(1-\alpha)\eta + \alpha s_c}{[(1-\alpha)\eta + \alpha](1-\alpha)}(w_c - p) + \frac{\alpha s_{\bar{c}}}{[(1-\alpha)\eta + \alpha](1-\alpha)}(w_{\bar{c}} - p)$$

$$- \frac{(1-\alpha)(\eta - 1) + s_c}{[(1-\alpha)\eta + \alpha](1-\alpha)}z_c - \frac{s_{\bar{c}}}{[(1-\alpha)\eta + \alpha](1-\alpha)}z_{\bar{c}}$$

$$+ \frac{s_{\bar{c}}}{(1-\alpha)\eta + \alpha}(g_{\bar{c}} - g_c),$$

(A1.21)

where $(w_c - p) \equiv w_r^c$, and

$$\frac{-Ew_{rc}}{(1-\alpha)} = \left[l_0 + \frac{(1-\alpha)\eta + \alpha\,\theta}{(1-\alpha)} \frac{\theta}{\alpha}\right]$$

(see equation A1.14).[33]

The *aggregate* competitive wage, w_{rc}, is obtained by setting $u = 0$ in equation (1.17), and using equation (A1.5) to substitute away for m. Thus

$$w_{rc} = -\left[(1-\alpha)l_0 + [(1-\alpha)\eta + \alpha]\frac{\theta}{\alpha}\right] + \bar{z}. \tag{A1.22}$$

Since (from equations A1.14 and A1.22) $E w_{rc} = w_{rc} - \bar{z}$, country c's unemployment in (A1.21) can be rewritten as

$$u_c = \frac{(1-\alpha)\eta + \alpha s_c}{[(1-\alpha)\eta + \alpha](1-\alpha)}(w_r^c - w_{rc})$$

$$+ \frac{\alpha s_{\bar{c}}}{[(1-\alpha)\eta + \alpha](1-\alpha)}(w_r^{\bar{c}} - w_{rc})$$

$$- \frac{(\eta - 1)s_{\bar{c}}}{(1-\alpha)\eta + \alpha}(z_c - z_{\bar{c}}) + \frac{s_{\bar{c}}}{(1-\alpha)\eta + \alpha}(g_{\bar{c}} - g_c). \tag{A1.23}$$

Thus u_c is a function of the differences between the *ex post* values of the actual real wage in each country and the *aggregate* competitive wage ($w_r^c - w_{rc}$ and $w_r^{\bar{c}} - w_{rc}$ respectively). Since, by definition, $w_r^c \equiv w^c - p$, the randomness associated with the real wage of each country depends entirely on the realization of the *aggregate* price level, p, in stage 3. From equation (1.13),

$$w_r^c \equiv w^c - p = w^c - [((1-\alpha)\eta + \alpha)\theta + \alpha\bar{w} + (1-\alpha)(m + \bar{g}) - \bar{z}].$$

$$\tag{A1.24}$$

Using equation (1.19) to substitute m away in (A1.24), we can rewrite the expression for w_r^c as

$$w_r^c = E(w_r^c) + \frac{1}{1 + (1-\alpha)^2 I}\bar{z}, \qquad c = 1, 2, \tag{A1.25}$$

where $E(w_r^c)$ is the expected real wage in country c. Combining the expression for $E(w_{rc})$ from equation (A1.14) with equation (A1.25), we obtain

$$w_r^c - w_{rc} = \left(E(w_r^c) + \frac{1}{1 + (1-\alpha)^2 I}\bar{z}\right) - (E(w_{rc}) + \bar{z})$$

$$= \phi_c - \left(\frac{(1-\alpha)^2 I}{1 + (1-\alpha)^2 I}\right)\bar{z}, \qquad c = 1, 2. \tag{A1.26}$$

After using equation (A1.26) to substitute away both $(w_r^c - w_{rc})$ and $(w_r^{\bar{c}} - w_{rc})$ in equation (A1.23) and rearranging, we obtain

$$
u_c = \left\{ \frac{(1-\alpha)\eta + \alpha s_c}{[(1-\alpha)\eta + \alpha](1-\alpha)} \phi_c + \frac{\alpha s_{\bar{c}}}{[(1-\alpha)\eta + \alpha](1-\alpha)} \phi_{\bar{c}} \right\}
$$

$$
- \left[\frac{(1-\alpha)I \, s_c}{1 + (1-\alpha)^2 I} + \frac{(\eta-1)s_{\bar{c}}}{[(1-\alpha)\eta + \alpha]} \right] \cdot z_c
$$

$$
- \left[\frac{(1-\alpha)I \, s_{\bar{c}}}{1 + (1-\alpha)^2 I} - \frac{(\eta-1)s_{\bar{c}}}{(1-\alpha)\eta + \alpha} \right] \cdot z_{\bar{c}}
$$

$$
+ \frac{s_{\bar{c}}}{(1-\alpha)\eta + \alpha}(g_{\bar{c}} - g_c), \qquad c = 1, 2. \tag{A1.27}
$$

Equation (1.35) in the text is obtained by rearranging equation (A1.27).

Note that although the aggregate shock $\bar{g} = s_1 g_1 + s_2 g_2$ is fully offset by the CB (see equation 1.19), the individual shocks g_1 and g_2 separately affect *each* country's rate of unemployment.

Notes

This chapter was presented at the CESifo, Yrjo Jahnsson Foundation conference on Issues of Monetary Integration in Europe, Munich, Germany, December 2000, at the CEPR/ INSEAD workshop in macroeconomics on The Design and Implementation of Monetary Policy, Fontainebleau, France, April 2001, and at the Universita degli Studi di Milano–Biccoca conference on EMU Macroeconomic Institutions, Milan, Italy, September 2001. We benefited from a critical remark, by Lars Svensson, on a previous version which led to some restructuring of the model in the chapter. We also would like to thank Petra Geraats, Erkki Koskela, Assaf Razin, David Romer, Alexander Wolman, and anonymous referees for useful comments.

1. An overview appears in Calmfors (2001). In some of the literature, the level of central bank conservativeness is found to have real effect only if unions are averse to inflation (Yashiv 1989; Gylfason and Lindbeck 1994; Jensen 1997; Skott 1997, Gruner and Hefeker 1999). The breakdown of monetary neutrality under inflation-aversion is not as surprising compared with the case where all individuals in the private sector care only about real variables.

2. In related work Gruner and Hefeker (1999) and Cukierman and Lippi (2001) analyze the real effects of the replacement of national monetary policies or an ERM by a monetary union. These effects are triggered by changes in the strategic interactions of unions with the CB. Lawler (2000) considers the effect of shocks in a closed unionized economy, and Lane (2000) considers the effect of shocks in an MU, but without explicit modeling of the behavior of unions and price-setting firms.

3. See also equations (1.10) and (1.11) below.

4. We will also occasionally refer to the parameter I as central bank conservativeness (CBC).

5. The permanent level of output in each country is defined as the equilibrium level of output in the absence of shocks. Those levels do not therefore depend on the realizations of shocks.

6. The constant values of (Y_1^p, Y_2^p) have been subsumed into the functional form of $F(.)$.

7. Although this specification is reminiscent of the demand for good j in Blanchard and Kiyotaki (1987), it is based on somewhat different underpinnings. Blanchard and Kiyotaki derive it from a particular utility function in a model with no interest rate. In our model the primitive is the demand facing firm j rather than utility, but the role of the interest rate in affecting demand is incorporated explicitly. In a previous version of this paper (Coricelli, Cukierman, and Dalmazzo 2001) we had postulated a variant of such a demand function as the primitive.

8. In that we deviate from much of the recent literature on the strategic interaction between unions and the CB, built on unions' inflation-aversion. A nonexhaustive list includes Jensen (1997), Skott (1997), Cukierman and Lippi (1999), Guzzo and Velasco (1999), Lippi (2000), Lawler (2000), and our own work in Coricelli, Cukierman and Dalmazzo (2000). The reason for this abstraction is that unions' concern about unemployment among their members is likely to be far more important than their fear of inflation.

9. The index j identifies the firm and the index i identifies the union that organizes that firm's labor force.

10. Using (1.8) in (1.9), we obtain the following alternative form of a typical firm's demand for labor

$$l_{ij}^{dc} = \kappa + \frac{1}{\alpha + \eta(1-\alpha)} \left[-\eta \left(w_i^c - p \right) + (m-p) + g_c + (\eta-1)z_c \right],$$

where $\kappa \equiv -\eta\theta/\alpha$. This alternative form implies that, other things the same, when the union manages to raise its real wage, the demand for labor by the firm goes down unless real money balances also increase.

11. More precisely, it is an average of the logarithms of nominal wages in country c.

12. Note, however, that a higher productivity level also raises the competitiveness of a country's products ($p_c - p$ goes down), which reduces unemployment by raising demand for the products of the country. This general equilibrium effect is incorporated into the analysis later.

13. The result that $\bar{z}$ has no net effect on employment is a specific feature of this model. In general, the effect of $\bar{z}$ on unemployment is likely to be small in comparison to its effect on inflation. As a consequence the reaction of the CB to the productivity shocks will be motivated by the desire to iron out fluctuations in inflation, even when the two opposite effects of $\bar{z}$ on employment do not exactly offset each other.

14. Econometric evidence appears in Cukierman, Rodriguez, and Webb (1998) and casual evidence in Hall (1994) and in Hall and Franzese (1998). Further details appear in subsection 2.2 of CCD (2000).

15. The expressions for the expected values of average unemployment and inflation in the MU are similar to those obtained in the closed economy model of CCD (2000) with country variables replaced by their MU aggregate counterparts. Compare equations (1.27) and (1.29) here with equations (24) and (25) in CCD (2000).

16. See section 1.6.3 of the appendix for a proof.

17. See section 1.6.4 of the appendix for a proof.

18. This mechanism is basically identical to that found in the closed economy framework in CCD (2000) for the case in which unions are not directly averse to inflation.

19. See section 1.6.5 of the appendix for a proof.

20. For further discussion of those channels the reader is referred to section 3.2 of CCD (2000).

21. Cukierman and Lippi (2001) rely on a similar mechanism, in the context of inflation averse labor unions, to argue that the formation of a MU will raise unions' wage aggressiveness by raising the number of unions playing against the single CB.

22. Equation (1.30) is obtained by applying the expected value operator to equation (A1.5) and using equations (A1.16) and (1.25).

23. The proof appears in section 1.6.6 of the appendix. Since the competitive real wages are the same in both countries all the statements made about expected wage premia in the preceding propositions also apply to expected real wages in both countries.

24. The proof is a direct consequence of the fact that $\partial q^c / \partial I < 0$ and $Eu^c = q^c / A$. The first relation is established in the proof of proposition 1.2 and the second in the proof of proposition 1.4. Both proofs appear in the appendix.

25. See also note 13.

26. From the monetary rule in equation (1.19), the variance of the money supply turns out to be

$$\text{var}(m) = E[m - E(m)]^2 = \frac{(1-\alpha)^2 I^2}{[1+(1-\alpha)^2 I]^2} \sigma_{\tilde{z}}^2 + \sigma_{\tilde{g}}^2.$$

Since $\partial \, \text{var}(m)/\partial I > 0$, the degree of activism in the management of money supply increases in CB conservativeness.

27. Equation (1.34) is obtained by substituting equation (A1.27) for $c = 1, 2$ into equation (1.16), and by rearranging.

28. The terms "populist" and "ultra liberal" to designate a CB with $I = 0$ are due, respectively, to Guzzo and Velasco (1999) and Cukierman and Lippi (1999).

29. Chprits (2001) utilizes the famework of this chapter to characterize economic performance in a pre-monetary union situation, in which one country (the follower) unilaterally pegs its exchange rate to the currency of the other country (the leader). She utilizes this framework to show that replacement of an EMS type system (in which the countries in the "follower" block unilaterally pegs their currencies to that of the leader country) by a monetary union affects real economic performance. In particular, other things the same, unemployment in the leading or core (follower or pheriphery) country is lower (higher) under EMU than under an EMS type system.

30. In related work for a single closed economy with many unions, Bratsiotis and Martin (1999) reach a similar conclusion using a framework in which the policy rule of the CB (rather than its objectives) is taken as the primitive. In a model with traded and non-traded goods Holden (1999) shows that the type of monetary regime (exchange rate rule vs. a price target) affects the composition of employment across sectors.

31. This trade-off is a generalized one since a more conservative CB is associated with better average performance not only with respect to inflation (as in Rogoff) but also with respect to unemployment.

32. A recent survey of New Keynesian models appears in Clarida, Gali, and Gertler (1999).

33. Note that w_c designates the nominal wage in country c, w_{rc} designates the MU-wide competitive real wage and w_r^c designates the competitive real wage in country c.

References

Barro, R. J., and R. Gordon. 1983. A positive theory of monetary policy in a natural rate model. *Journal of Political Economy* 91: 589–610.

Berger, H., and U. Woitek. 1999. Does conservatism matter? A time series approach to central banking. Working Paper 190, CESifo, June.

Blanchard, O., and N. Kiyotaki. 1987. Monopolistic competition and the effects of aggregate demand. *American Economic Review* 77: 647–66.

Blanchard, O., and S. Fischer. 1989. *Lectures in Macroeconomics.* Cambridge: MIT Press.

Bratsiotis, G., and C. Martin. 1999. Stabilization, policy targets and unemployment in imperfectly competitive economies. *Scandinavian Journal of Economics* 101: 241–56.

Calmfors, L. 1998. Monetary Union and precautionary labor market reform. Seminar Paper 659, IIES, Stockholm University.

Calmfors, L. 2001a. Unemployment, labor market reform and Monetary Union. *Journal of Labor Economics* 19: 265–89.

Calmfors, L. 2001b. Wages and wage-bargaining institutions in the EMU—A survey of the issues. Seminar Paper 690, IIES, Stockholm University.

Chprits, E. 2001. Monetary Union versus alternative exchange rate regimes: Analysis of economic performance. Unpublished Master thesis. Berglas School of Economics, Tel-Aviv University. November.

Clarida R., J. Gali, and M. Gertler. 1999. The science of monetary policy: A new Keynesian perspective. *Journal of Economic Literature* 37: 1661–1707.

Coricelli, F., A. Cukierman, and A. Dalmazzo. 2000. Monetary institutions, monopolistic competition, unionized labor markets and economic performance. CEPR Discussion Paper 2407. March. Available at: *http://www.tau.ac.il/~alexcuk/pdf/ccd-av3.pdf.*

Coricelli, F., A. Cukierman, and A. Dalmazzo. 2001. Economic performance and stabilization policy in a Monetary Union with imperfect labour and goods markets. CEPR Discussion Paper 2745. March.

Cukierman, A., and F. Lippi. 1999. Central Bank independence, centralization of wage bargaining, inflation and unemployment—Theory and some evidence. *European Economic Review* 43: 1395–1434. Available at: *http://www.tau.ac.il/~alexcuk/pdf/Lippi1EER.pdf.*

Cukierman, A., and F. Lippi. 2001. Labour markets and Monetary Union: A strategic analysis. *Economic Journal* 111: 541–65. Available at: *http://www.tau.ac.il/~alexcuk/pdf/LipiEMU799.pdf.*

Cukierman, A., P. Rodriguez, and S. Webb. 1998. Central Bank autonomy and exchange rate regimes—Their effects on monetary accommodation and activism. In S. Eijffinger H. Huizinga, eds., *Positive Political Economy—Theory and Evidence*. Cambridge: Cambridge University Press.

Flanagan, R. J., D. W. Soskice, and L. Ulman. 1983. *Unionism, Economic Stabilization, and Income Policies: European Experience*. Washington, DC: Brookings Institution.

Franzese, R. J., Jr. 2000. Credibly conservative monetary policy and wage/price–bargaining organization: A review with implications for monetary policy in the European common currency area. Center for Political Studies, Institute for Social Research, University of Michigan.

Gasiorek, M. 2000. Product markets and monetary union. Paper presented at the CEPR/ESI Conference on *Vivent Les Differences? Heterogeneous Europe*. Amsterdam, September 2000.

Gruner, H. P., and C. Hefeker. 1999. How will EMU affect inflation and unemployment in Europe? *Scandinavian Journal of Economics* 101: 33–47.

Guzzo, V., and A. Velasco. 1999. The case for a populist Central Bank. *European Economic Review* 43: 1317–44.

Gylfason, T., and A. Lindbeck. 1994. The interaction of monetary policy and wages. *Public Choice* 79: 33–46.

Hall, P. A. 1994. Central Bank independence and coordinated wage bargaining: Their interaction in Germany and Europe. *German Politics and Society* (31): 1–23.

Hall, P. A., and R. J. Franzese Jr. 1998. Mixed signals: Central Bank independence, coordinated wage bargaining, and European Monetary Union. *International Organization* 52: 505–35.

Holden, S. 1999. Wage setting under different monetary regimes. Memorandum 12/99, University of Oslo.

Holden, S. 2001. Monetary regimes and the co-ordination of wage setting. CESifo Working Paper 429. *European Economic Review*, forthcoming.

Jensen, H. 1997. Monetary policy cooperation may not be counterproductive. *Scandinavian Journal of Economics* 99: 73–80.

Kydland, F. E., and E. C. Prescott. 1977. Rules rather than discretion: The inconsistency of optimal plans. *Journal of Political Economy* 85: 473–92.

Lane, P. 2000. Asymmetric shocks and monetary policy in a currency union. *Scandinavian Journal of Economics* 102: 585–604.

Lawler, P. 2000. Centralised wage setting, inflation contracts, and the optimal choice of central banker. *Economic Journal* 110: 559–75.

Lippi, F. 1999. Strategic monetary policy with non-atomistic wage setters: A case for non-neutrality. CEPR Discussion Paper 2218. August.

Lippi, F. 2002. Revisiting the case for a populist central banker. *European Economic Review* 46: 601–12.

Nickell, S. 1997. Unemployment and labor market rigidities: Europe versus North America. *Journal of Economic Perspectives* 11: 55–74.

Nickell, S. 1999. Product markets and labour markets. *Labour Economics* 6: 1–20.

OECD. 1997. *Employment Outlook*. Paris. July.

Oswald, A. J. 1982. The microeconomic theory of trade union. *Economic Journal* 92: 576–95.

Rogoff, K. 1985. The optimal degree of commitment to a monetary target. *Quarterly Journal of Economics* 100: 1169–90.

Sibert, A. 1999. Monetary integration and economic reform. *Economic Journal* 109: 78–92.

Sibert, A., and A. Sutherland. 2000. Monetary Union and labor market reform. *Journal of International Economics* 51: 421–35.

Skott, P. 1997. Stagflationary consequences of prudent monetary policy in a unionized economy. *Oxford Economic Papers* 49: 609–22.

Soskice, D., and T. Iversen. 2000. The non neutrality of monetary policy with large price or wage setters. *Quarterly Journal of Economics* 115: 265–84.

Yashiv, E. 1989. Inflation and the role of money under discretion and rules. Working Paper 8-89. MIT. November.

Comment on Chapter 1

Erkki Koskela

The extension of the closed economy model by Coricelli, Cukierman, and Dalmazzo (2000) allows for open economy interactions as well as demand and productivity shocks. The authors analyze various aspects of the economic performance, in the Monetary Union, of unionized labor markets, monopolistically competitive price-setting firms, and stabilization policy in the presence of demand and productivity shocks (both aggregate and country specific). More precisely, they explore the effects of centralized wage bargaining, or CWB (i.e., inverse of the number of trade unions), product market competition (i.e., price elasticity of goods demand), and conservative central bank strategies (i.e., the relative weight of inflation in its loss function) on average economic performance of the Monetary Union. They also study under various types of shocks the Monetary Union's optimal stabilization policy, due to the central bank.

The basic framework they postulate is a four-stage game (or a tree-stage game if we "eliminate" the realized shocks) with two countries under the time sequence of decisions shown in figure 1.1. The game is solved in reverse order by using backward induction. The authors consider a production function with productivity shocks, a demand function with demand shocks, and assume that the central bank (CB) is interested in preventing both inflation and unemployment, whereas national trade unions want real wages but dislike unemployment.

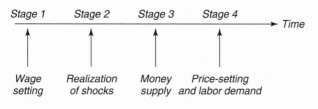

Figure 1.1

On the properties of the four stages of the game, in the stage 4, labor demand depends negatively on the real wage and positively on the demand for goods, and both of these factors will have a positive effect on the price setting. In stage 3 of the game, the common CB determines nominal money supply (or interest rate) by taking into account the effect of this choice on the price level. CB is assumed to minimize the loss function given the nominal wages, the various types of realized and anticipated shocks. The authors show that the CB's reaction function is a linear function of the average nominal wage rate and the average level of productivity and demand shocks in the monetary union. CB's conservatism matters: if conservatism is high enough, a rise in the average wage rate will lead to a fall in the nominal money supply. In stage 2 of the game, demand and productivity shocks are realized, and in stage 1, national trade unions in both countries choose nominal wage rates in a Nash fashion prior to the realization of shocks, as this way they minimize the expected losses from unemployment and a low real wage. In the model the wage rates are above the level of those in a competitive labor market (i.e., the wage premium is positive) and real wages in the two countries are strategic substitutes in the sense that when the real wage rate in one country is higher, the real wage chosen by the other country is lower, ceteris paribus.

Now I would like to mention the following implications of the model: (1) A rise in competitiveness of product markets (measured by the higher price elasticity of goods demand) and a rise in CB's conservativeness lead to lower expected values of the average wage premium, lower unemployment, and lower inflation in the monetary union, while the reverse happens when the CWB decreases (i.e., the number of unions increases). The intuition in the first case is clear. Higher competitiveness and higher CB's conservativeness lead to moderate wages. In the second case the argument is similar to the "corporatism" hypothesis of Calmfors and Driffill. (2) Among the countries with the same degree of centralization of wage bargaining, the smaller country (i.e., with a smaller number of firms) has a higher expected rate of unemployment, while among countries close in size, the country with more centralized wage bargaining has a lower expected rate of unemployment. These findings mean that despite any common monetary policy, unemployment and competitiveness may differ across countries even in the absence of shocks, and that equilibrium unemployment will fall as the CB's conservatism and the centralization of wage bargaining increase. (3) As for stabilization policy, the authors show that CB fully offsets the effect of aggregate demand shocks on the monetary union, since these shocks do not require the CB to compromise reducing inflation variability with employment variability. Moreover, as the CB accommodates the MU-wide average productivity shocks but allows some of the aggregate productivity shocks to affect inflation, the more conservative CB becomes more activist.

Clearly, this is a very important study. It is well written, the intuition is fully explained, and it unifies the existing literature with several interesting results. I have only two small comments, which can be considered topics for further research.

First, the way competitiveness is modeled in the product market is problematic. The authors' starting point is to use a Dixit-Stiglitz type model of monopolistic competition, where the markup price depends on the price elasticity of the demanded goods, and this in turn depends on exogenous preferences. Economic integration, however, certainly means something else. The degree of competitiveness in the goods market does not depend on exogenous preferences but rather on the impact of changes in economic integration. From this point of view there are at least two ways to model change in competitiveness: either by postulating that trade costs change or that new markets emerge for the firms as a result of higher economic integration (e.g., see Andersen and Sorensen 2000). The question to explore then is: What is the relationship of the Monetary Union to the degree of economic integration and equilibrium unemployment when economic integration is modeled endogenously?

Second, it has been recently argued in a convincing way that the best way to understand European unemployment over the last thirty years is to consider the interaction between economic shocks and labor market institutions (e.g., see Blanchard and Wolfers 2000). The unanswered question is whether optimal stabilization policy depends on labor market institutions. Exploration of this issue would require a model of the dynamic aspects associated with unemployment hysteresis.

References

Andersen, T. M., and J. R. Sorensen. 2000. Product market integration and wage formation. *Journal of Economic Integration* 15: 281–93.

Blanchard, O., and J. Wolfers. 2000. The role of shocks and institutions in the rise of European unemployment: The aggregate evidence. *Economic Journal*, 110: C1–C33.

Coricelli, F., A. Cukierman, and A. Dalmazzo. 2000. Monetary institutions, monopolistic competition, unionized labour markets and economic performance. CEPR Discussion Paper 2407. March.

2 Asymmetric Transmission of Monetary Policy: What Should the ECB Do If One Size Does Not Fit All?

Daniel Gros
and Carsten Hefeker

2.1 Introduction

In any monetary union there will be differences between regions in terms of economic performance, as figure 2.1 shows. Should the monetary authority react to these divergences? For the euro area, the standard answer is no: the ECB is held responsible for the average performance of the entire euro zone. However, as in some countries the performance starts to diverge considerably from the average, this answer appears superficial. It is not satisfactory because it does not take into account that the EU was created to serve the interests of its member states, which remain the basic political units in Europe. This differentiates the euro area from nation states, even very federally organized ones, in which the main political unit coincides with the monetary union. Therefore, countries whose performance is far from the average would not be served appropriately by such a policy.

The issue of what should be the political unit whose welfare should be taken into account by the ECB is important because welfare is usually assumed to be a concave function of economic performance. To use a concrete example, imagine a monetary union of two regions/countries of equal size. If we assume, as is usually done in the literature, that welfare losses are increasing in deviations of employment and inflation from their target levels, the countries are more strongly hurt are those where the unemployment rate is 10 percent as opposed to 2 percent, and the same applies to inflation. If the common central bank, however, only looks at averages over the entire union, which in this case would be 6 percent, the large welfare loss in one country would tend to be accounted for insufficiently. For the second country instead a monetary policy tailored to 6 percent unemployment would probably be too

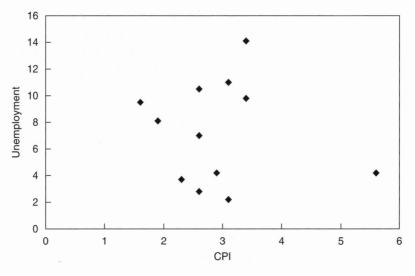

Figure 2.1
CPI inflation and unemployment for EU-12.

activist. Thus both countries would experience a welfare loss from a monetary policy that looks at averages.

Average welfare losses thus increase with the dispersion of unemployment. But in a monetary union it is impossible to have a nationally differentiated monetary policy. One is thus tempted to conclude that the ECB might deplore national divergences within the euro area, but that there is nothing it can, or should, do about them. This conclusion is, however, rash if one admits that monetary policy involves, at least in the short run, a trade-off between two policy goals: inflation and employment. In this case very high national unemployment rates enter the objective function with a de facto higher weight because they are squared. For current problems the question is whether to consider the unemployment rate of Spain (which is about one-half higher than the euro area average) as just one element in the calculation of the average areawide unemployment or as the high welfare losses it causes in Spain separately. The situation in Spain would presumably affect decisions by the ECB much more under the second approach.

The deeper issue is thus what should the ECB do when one size clearly does not fit all? Should it base its decisions on the areawide averages of inflation and unemployment, or should it attempt to minimize the (weighted) average of national welfare losses resulting from actual national inflation and unemployment rates? In this chapter we aim to provide a first step toward an answer by showing to what extend these two choices would lead to different policies in a world where the preferences regarding inflation and unemployment are identical, but where there are differences in the monetary transition mechanism.

We thus go beyond the existing literature, where it is usually assumed that the common central bank bases its decision only on unionwide state variables (Alesina and Grilli 1992). The literature on central bank constitutions for monetary unions, in contrast, assumes the same for the centrally appointed members of the decision-making body, whereas the representatives appointed by the constituting regions of the monetary union are assumed to look only at the welfare losses of their home region (von Hagen and Süppel 1994; Aksoy, de Grauwe, and Dewachter 2002). But both strands of the existing literature do not deal with the problem discussed here, namely how a homogeneous body of decision makers in the ECB council should set monetary policy. The study closest to ours is De Grauwe (2000) who addresses the same question. With a two-country model he arrives at similar conclusions using a series of simulations. Our more general formulation allows us to derive general analytical results in a multiple-country setting.

The next section presents the model used for the analysis. We use a standard model because we want to draw attention to the general point that there is a difference between area-wide welfare based on the (weighted) areawide averages of national performances and the average areawide welfare based on (also weighted) national welfare, which arises in the standard approach but has been neglected so far. Section 2.3 calculates the policy resulting under both choices (in the form of reaction functions), while section 2.4 draws welfare conclusions for the entire union and individual countries. Section 2.5 concludes.

2.2. The Model

We use a standard model, based on the usual two building blocks, a labor demand function and a welfare function defined over inflation and employment. We assume that there are $j = 1 \ldots N$ member countries in the monetary union.

Labor demand in country j is given as

$$n_j = \alpha_j \left(\pi_j - \pi_j^e \right) + \varepsilon_j + \rho_j \xi, \tag{2.1}$$

where ε_j is a pure national shock with $E(\varepsilon) = 0$ and $E(\varepsilon_j^2) = \sigma_{\varepsilon_j}^2$. As the ε_j's represent national asymmetric shocks, we assume that the covariances among them are equal to zero. To the extent that the national shocks are correlated, their covariance should show up in a higher variance of the common shock ξ. It could best be thought of as a worldwide commodity shock, a global recession, or a shock to the external exchange rate. The latter thus captures truly common shocks plus any covariance among national shocks. For the common shock we likewise assume $E(\xi) = 0$ and $E(\xi^2) = \sigma_\xi^2$ and that the common shock is not correlated to national shocks $E(\varepsilon_j \xi) = 0$.

We allow for the common shocks to affect different countries differently, as expressed by the subscript j for the parameter ρ_j. For example, an increase in the oil price would affect all euro area countries, but it would affect those countries more that are more dependent on energy-intensive sectors. We are not interested in the absolute size of the impact of the common shock on different national economies but only the *relative* one, namely the differences across countries. The parameter ρ_j shows thus the impact of a common shock for each country relative to the average impact. (One implications of this, which will be used later, is that the average of the ρ_j's over all countries is equal to one.)

Finally, the parameter α_j measures the employment effects of monetary policy in country j. In what follows we refer to this as the transmission mechanism of monetary policy.

The labor demand function we have chosen here is the most simple form that one can imagine for the purpose at hand. An alternative formulation would be the derivation of a model in the neo-Keynesian tradition with explicit IS-LM curves (e.g., see Clarida et al. 1999; Svensson 2001). We are fully aware that this is a simplification, but it has the definitive advantage of being very simple. In addition this simple workhorse model can most easily be compared to the relevant literature, cited above, that uses similar setups. The general result of our simple model will moreover carry over to more complicated setups.

Preferences of the (welfare-maximizing) authorities are formulated as a loss function $\Omega_j = E_{t-1}[\sum_{t=1}^{\infty} \beta^{t-1} L_{j,t}]$, where $L_{j,t}$ is the per period loss function. Because all periods are ex ante identical we drop the time index and are only interested in the current loss, which is specified (all variables are expressed as logs) in the usual way:

$$L_j = b(n_j - k_j)^2 + \pi_j^2, \tag{2.2}$$

where b is the relative weight country j puts on the employment aim, k_j expresses the level of distortions on the labor market that keep employment below its full employment level (Barro and Gordon 1983; Rogoff 1985). As usual, it is assumed that employment is below its potential due to the influence of strong labor unions that use their power to push wages above the market-clearing level. If labor unions are characterized by a separation into insiders and outsiders, the former will set wages too high for full employment. Unemployed outsiders have no influence on wage setting.

All of this is standard, and so is the problem for the monetary authority, namely to minimize the one-period loss. We emphasize that the parameter b does not have a subscript because we assume that preferences (i.e., inflation aversion) are identical in all countries, as we want to see whether divergences in national performance should influence the decisions of the ECB even if preferences are identical.

More recently a discussion has begun about the merit of this assumption. It has been claimed that central banks do not, in fact aim at increasing employment above its natural level and that therefore this model is beyond reality (Blinder 1998). We do not fully accept this argument, however. For one, the mere fact that central bank independence is considered necessary implies that the problem must be taken seriously. Central bank independence is seen as a solution to the problem, and if it is successful, this does not mean the problem does not exist.[1] The mere fact that the United States does not seem to have a credibility problem does not imply that the problem is not important. But, even if one were not willing to accept this idea, Jensen (2001) argues that the potential of a credibility problem is enough for the problem to exist. Apart from this, none of our results depend on this assumption. Even without a potential credibility problem, we derive interesting results.

In addition we measure independence by the parameter b, and not in the existence of the employment aim k. Only a b of zero, as Rogoff (1985) has shown, entirely solves the credibility problem, but at the price of excessive variability of employment.

2.3 Monetary Policy

We now proceed to calculate the optimal monetary policy under two different assumptions about the objective function of the ECB. We could minimize the (weighted) average of national losses or alternatively minimize the loss function calculated at the euro area level, using the (weighted) averages of national inflation rates and output gaps as input.

We have chosen these two setups because they best reflect the different institutional solutions for the formation of the ECB. A natural way of allocating preferences of large countries is by the weighted summation of welfare, in the tradition of a Benthamite-welfare function. This would correspond to the first mechanism that could be chosen to aggregate preferences. On the other hand, by its statutes and its rhetoric, the ECB is held to look at European developments only, without placing particular value on any single member country. Obviously, in deriving the aggregate figures for euroland, the ECB will do this according to the relative weight of this country. This is the second setup that we consider in this section. How either of the two mechanisms can actually be enforced is an issue that we return to below.

2.3.1 Minimizing National Welfare Losses

The union monetary authority maximizes the weighted average of national utilities. This leads to the following program:

$$\text{minimize } L = \sum_j \mu_j \lfloor b(n_j - k_j)^2 + \pi^2 \rfloor, \tag{2.3}$$

where the relative weight of country j is μ_j, with $\sum_j \mu_j = 1$. In equation (2.3) we have already used the fact that in our one good model inflation is the same all over the monetary union. This implies that our model cannot replicate one of the problems facing the ECB, namely divergences in national inflation rates. Different national inflation rates could, for example, arise in a model with nontradables and tradables in the presence of the Balass-Samuelson effect. We abstract from this complication, however. The majority of EMU members, in particular the larger countries, have inflation rates relatively close together.

For convenience, we make simplifying assumptions concerning the shocks to employment. To simplify notation, we define averages with an upper bar and assume that $\sum_j \mu_j \varepsilon_j = \bar{\varepsilon} = 0$ and $\sum_j \mu_j \rho_j = \bar{\rho} = 1$.

Using (2.1) in (2.3) and minimizing this expression with respect to the (common) rate of inflation and imposing rational expectations, the rate of inflation is

$$\pi^N = b \sum_j \mu_j \alpha_j k_j - \frac{b \sum_j \mu_j \alpha_j (\rho_j \xi + \varepsilon_j)}{1 + b \sum_j \mu_j \alpha_j^2}, \tag{2.4}$$

where the superscript N denotes the case of monetary policy based on national welfare. Inflation is increasing in the size of the distortion in all member economies (the inflation bias) and in response to a common shock.

For better comparability with further results we note that $\sum_j \mu_j \alpha_j k_j = \theta_{\alpha,k} + \bar{\alpha} \bar{k}^2$ and that $b \sum_j \mu_j \alpha_j^2 = b(\theta_\alpha^2 + \bar{\alpha}^2)$.[3] In addition we have assumed, for simplicity, that there is no systematic correlation between the ρ_j's and the α's. (In the notation of note 2 this could be written as: $\theta_{\alpha,\rho} = 0$.) Relaxing this assumption would lead to an additional element in the welfare comparisons performed below, but it would not affect our central point, namely that there is a difference between looking at the average performance or taking national welfare functions into account.

With this notation the rate of inflation, when the central bank cares about national welfare, can be rewritten

$$\pi^N = b(\theta_{\alpha,k} + \bar{\alpha}\bar{k}) - \frac{b\bar{\alpha}}{1 + b(\theta_\alpha^2 + \bar{\alpha}^2)}\xi \equiv b(\theta_{\alpha,k} + \bar{\alpha}\bar{k}) - \Omega^N \xi, \qquad (2.4')$$

with $\Omega^N > 0$ denoting the reaction to the common shock.

2.3.2 Minimizing Areawide Welfare Losses Based on National Performance

Alternatively, the ECB might base its decision on an areawide utility function that uses the averages of national rates of employment and inflation as input. The problem then becomes

$$\text{minimize } L = b \left[\sum_j \mu_j (n_j - k_j) \right]^2 + \pi^2. \qquad (2.5)$$

Substituting in equation (2.1) for employment, taking the first-order condition, and imposing rational expectations, we rewrite inflation for this case as

$$\pi^A = b\bar{\alpha}\bar{k} - \frac{b\bar{\alpha}\xi}{1 + b\bar{\alpha}^2} \equiv b\bar{\alpha}\bar{k} - \Omega^A \xi, \qquad (2.6)$$

where we have used again the fact that $\sum_j \mu_j = 1$, that $\sum_j \mu_j k_j \equiv \bar{k}$ and that the average idiosyncratic shock is zero. The reaction parameter to the shock is defined as $\Omega^A > 0$. The superscript A denotes the case of monetary policy being tailored to area wage averages of national performances. Inflation is again increasing in the average size of the distortion in the member economies (the inflation bias) and in response to the common shock.

2.3.3 A Comparison of Inflation Rates

In the next step we explore what influence the difference in the objective function of the central bank in the two alternative cases would have. Comparing equations (2.4) and (2.6) reveals that the difference between the two solutions stems from two sources. First the inflation bias, resulting from the aggregation of national distortions, is different in the two cases. The second difference lies in the strength of the reaction to the common shock. Comparing equations (2.4′) and (2.6) shows that $\Omega^N < \Omega^A$ for a positive θ_α^2.

From these results we can compare the rates of inflation in the two cases

$$\pi^N - \pi^A = b\theta_{\alpha,k} + \frac{\bar{\alpha}b^2\theta^2}{\left(1 + b\left(\bar{\alpha}^2 + \theta_\alpha^2\right)\right)\left(1 + \bar{\alpha}^2 b\right)}\xi. \tag{2.7}$$

It is thus not possible to say whether a central bank that addresses its policy to national objectives will produce a higher inflation bias. This will be the case only if there is a positive relation between the effectiveness of monetary policy and the level of distortions $\theta_{\alpha,k} > 0$. However, a central bank that minimizes (the average of national) welfare losses will in general stabilize aggregate shocks less (the second term being positive). The overall effect on the rate of inflation is thus indeterminate.

The intuition behind the result that the rate of inflation is higher under the national welfare-maximizing monetary regime—if there is a positive relation between the two key parameters, the effectiveness of monetary policy and labor market distortions—is the following: The more effective monetary policy is (a high α), the lower the marginal costs of using monetary policy. If in this situation distortions (k) are also high, the central bank has a higher incentive to use active monetary policy. This problem is magnified by the fact that the central bank cares for national welfare instead of averages. In this case countries with a high level of distortions are strongly taken into account. Since this is known to rational private agents, the expected rate of inflation increases; hence a higher inflation bias results. If, on the other hand, α and k are negatively related, the result is reversed, and the inflation bias is lower. Actually there are arguments that would suggest that the relation between k

and α is indeed negative. If distortions in an economy are structurally high, there is a well-known incentive to fight this problem with an active monetary policy; in other words, the time-consistency problem of monetary policy is high. Where this is the case, we can expect that agents take precaution not to be surprised by monetary policy. They will sign only short-term contracts or index wages and other payments to the rate of inflation. Then inflation should have only little impact on output and employment (Gray 1976). This would imply that α is small in cases where k is high.

This part, also important for the quantitative difference between the two rates of inflation, is not the only difference. Thus even if, as some claim, there is no inflation bias in the policy of the central bank, implying that this first term would be zero, a difference remains. This stems from the fact that the central bank will also react differently to shocks under the two decision-making mechanisms. In particular, it will take into account that the impact of monetary policy differs in the member countries, according to the size of the differences in the monetary policy transmission mechanism, when it looks at national welfare losses. This implies that for some countries much less monetary policy is necessary to stabilize shocks, whereas for others more would be needed. But since only one common monetary policy can be set, the central bank is required to balance these influences, leading in the end to the result that common shocks are stabilized less because a stronger reaction would hurt some countries more than they would gain. In other words, the ECB becomes more cautious in using monetary policy to stabilize shocks.

As differences in the transmission mechanism play a key role in our results, the questions thus arises how important these are in reality. The literature on this point is difficult to interpret because the underlying question has usually been different from ours. Some maintain the differences in the transmission mechanism are so large that they will make the operation of EMU difficult (Cecchetti 1999). Differences in financial and industrial structures as well as in the institutional setups imply that changes in the monetary policy lead to different effects in member countries. The same is true of differences in the banking systems and the varying importance of bank credit in the financing of private firms, in collateral requirements, and in the balance sheet of households.

Others argue that these differences in financial structures will diminish over time as countries share a common monetary policy (Dornbusch, Favero, and Giavazzi 1998). Most empirical studies concur, however, that

Table 2.1
Differences in the transmission mechanism

Country	Impact on output of 1 percent increase in interest rates (absolute changes)
EMU members	
Belgium	0.72
France	1.30
Germany	1.21
Ireland	0.76
Italy	0.64
Portugal	0.39
Spain	0.46
EMU nonmembers	
Denmark	0.48
Sweden	0.56
United Kingdom	0.53

Source: Cecchetti 1999.

at present there are still large differences in the transmission mechanism, although they are difficult to estimate precisely (e.g., see Borio 1995; Gerlach and Smets 1995; Eijffinger and de Haan 2000; Angeloni et al. 2001; Mihov 2001). Table 2.1 reports the estimates from Cecchetti (1999) that suggest the differences in the output multiplier to be considerable. The highest coefficient is over three times larger than the lowest. There is thus some evidence that differences in the transmission mechanisms are large.

2.4   A Welfare Comparison

2.4.1   Unionwide Welfare

Having derived the difference in inflation and in the stabilization of shocks under the two alternative objective functions for the common central bank, it remains to be seen what welfare implications this would have.

As the comparison of welfare under the alternative regime should be done on an ex ante basis, we concentrate on expected welfare losses. We start with an evaluation of the average welfare of all union members; that is, we use $L = \sum_j \mu_j L_j$ as our measure for the average welfare within the union. Of course, this is only one of many possible ways of aggregating welfare within euroland. It is a natural starting point, however, since it reflects the simple weighted sum of welfare within countries.[4]

In the case that the common central bank cares for averages, we have expected losses for the entire union of (after using equation (2.1) to substitute out for employment)

$$E[L^A] = E\left[b \sum_j \mu_j(-\alpha_j\Omega^A\xi + \rho_j\xi + \varepsilon_j - k_j)^2 + (b\bar{\alpha}\bar{k} - \Omega^A\xi)^2 \right]. \quad (2.8)$$

Likewise the expected loss under the alternative is

$$E[L^N] = b \sum_j \mu_j[-\alpha_j\Omega^N\xi + \rho_j\xi + \varepsilon_j - k_j]^2 + [b(\theta_{\alpha,k} + \bar{\alpha}\bar{k}) - \Omega^N\xi]^2.$$

$$(2.9)$$

Multiplying out the quadratic terms and taking expectations, we write the difference as

$$E[L^A] - E[L^N] = \left\{ b \sum_j \mu_j(\rho_j - \alpha_j\Omega^A)^2 + (\Omega^A)^2 \right.$$

$$\left. - \left[b \sum_j \mu_j(\rho_j - \alpha_j\Omega^N)^2 + (\Omega^N)^2 \right] \right\} \sigma_\xi^2$$

$$- b^2\sigma_{\alpha,k}[\overline{2\alpha k} + \theta_{\alpha,k}]. \quad (2.10)$$

On average, the members of the monetary union can be thus better off under a common central bank that minimizes national welfare losses, as the first term in (2.10) is positive given that $\Omega^N < \Omega^A$. This first result is not surprising: the average of national welfare losses should be lower under a central bank that explicitly attempts to minimize the losses than under a central bank that does not. What is not so evident is that the gain from having the ECB look at national losses is increasing in the variance of the common shock σ_ξ^2. As we have already argued above, this reflects the fact that ECB now takes into account that different countries have a different need for active monetary policy in reaction to a *common* shock. It will therefore stabilize less, which is beneficial for the average country. Obviously the gain from this regime is thus larger, the higher the variance of the common shock. The effect is strengthened if the (common) dispersion of the α_j's increases.

This can be seen by rewriting (2.10), by using the definitions made above, as

$$E[L^A] - E[L^N] = (\Omega^A - \Omega^N) \left\{ \left(1 + b \left(\theta_\alpha^2 + \bar{\alpha}^2\right)\right) (\Omega^A + \Omega^N) - 2\bar{\alpha}\bar{b} \right\} \sigma_\xi^2$$
$$- b^2 \theta_{\alpha,k} [\bar{\alpha}\bar{k} + \theta_{\alpha,k}]. \tag{2.10'}$$

The second term of (2.10') expresses the fact that the inflation bias might be higher whenever the central bank cares for national welfare rather than average welfare. This is the case if the relation between the effectiveness of monetary policy and distortions is positive. As argued above, in this situation the central bank has a higher incentive to use active monetary policy, thus pushing up the expected rate of inflation. If, on the other hand, $\theta_{\alpha,k} < 0$, the result is reversed, and countries are clearly better off under a central bank that maximizes national welfare. But even if there is no systematic component in inflation due to the time-consistency problem, we see that the aggregation of preferences does make a difference to the average welfare of countries within Euroland.

2.4.2 Individual Country Welfare

Now if union member countries are *on average* better off under a common central bank that looks at national welfare, this does not necessarily imply that every country is better off in this situation. Dropping the summation in (2.10), the welfare comparison for any single country yields:

$$E\left[L_j^A\right] - E\left[L_j^N\right] = \{b(\rho_j - \alpha_j\Omega^A)^2 + (\Omega^A)^2 - \lfloor b(\rho_j - \alpha_j\Omega^N)^2 + (\Omega^N)^2 \rfloor\}\sigma_\xi^2$$
$$- b^2 \theta_{\alpha,k} [2\bar{\alpha}\bar{k}^2 + \theta_{\alpha,k}]. \tag{2.11}$$

For any individual country the welfare difference under two policy options for the common central bank remains thus the sum of the differences in the inflation bias and the stabilization to common shocks.

Again, the difference in welfare stems from two sources: the reaction to the common shocks and the inflation bias. The reaction to the common shock affects country j to the extent that it is hit by the common shock according to a country specific influence ρ_j. Taking the derivative of (2.11) with respect to ρ_j, we see that this is negative, meaning that country j prefers a central bank that looks at national developments if it is strongly affected by the common shock. If, instead, the country is not at all affected by the common shock, it would be better off with an averaging central bank.

The inflation bias term is unchanged and remains, as discussed above, a function of the relation $\theta_{\alpha,k}$. Since we do not have any information about this relation, it may be more promising to focus on the stabilization role of monetary policy and ask how the transmission mechanism determines under which regime a country would fare better.[5] We thus set $\theta_{\alpha,k} = 0$ and focus on the first term in (2.11).

Obviously this term is a function of α_j only. We begin by setting $\alpha_j = 0$, in which case the first term would clearly be positive given that $\Omega_A > \Omega_N$. The country would hence gain if the central bank should care for national welfare. Since monetary policy in this country is assumed to be ineffective ($\alpha_j = 0$), it loses from an active monetary policy; inflation variability would increase without any gain in terms of lower output variability. Thus the less the common central bank stabilizes, the better it is for such a country. The same is true if $\alpha_j \rightarrow \infty$ because then the first term would also be clearly positive, as long as α_j does not completely dominate $\bar{\alpha}$.[6] In this case monetary policy would be supereffective, and the country would prefer a less stabilizing central bank as moderate monetary policy would be sufficient. Otherwise, output variability would increase by too much for this country.

Hence the regime preferred by country j is a nonlinear function of its own α_j. To derive the critical $\tilde{\alpha}_j$ at which the country would just be indifferent with respect to the objectives of the common central, we set the first term in (2.11) equal to zero so that $(\rho_j - \alpha_j \Omega^A)^2 + (\Omega^A)^2 = (\rho_j - \alpha_j \Omega^N)^2 + (\Omega^N)^2$. The critical $\tilde{\alpha}_j$ is thus implicitly determined by

$$\frac{\tilde{\alpha}_j}{1 + \tilde{\alpha}_j^2} = \frac{\Omega^A + \Omega^N}{2\rho_j} = b\bar{\alpha} \frac{1 + b(\bar{\alpha}^2 + \theta_\alpha^2/2)}{\rho_j \left[1 + b(\bar{\alpha}^2 + \theta_\alpha^2)\right](1 + \bar{\alpha}^2 b)}. \tag{2.12}$$

There are then two solution for $\tilde{\alpha}_j$ that fulfill this condition (see figure 2.2), holding all other variables constant. To find the maximum of the function $\tilde{\alpha}_j/(1 + \tilde{\alpha}_j^2)$, we set $\partial[\tilde{\alpha}_j/(1 + \tilde{\alpha}_j^2)]/\partial\tilde{\alpha}_j = (1 - \tilde{\alpha}_j^2)/(1 + \tilde{\alpha}_j^2)^2$ equal to zero. This is the case at $\tilde{\alpha}_j = 1$. Ω^A and Ω^N are both negative functions of α_j as well because the individual α_j influences the average $\bar{\alpha}$. However, if the monetary union is sufficiently large, this influence will be of limited importance. If we, in addition, assume that the dispersion of all α's, θ_α^2, is unaffected by a variation in α_j, the RHS of the equality is a weakly declining function of α_j.

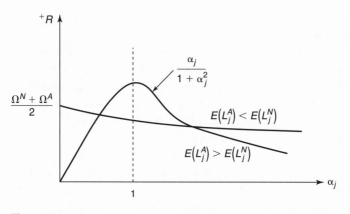

Figure 2.2
The critical $\tilde{\alpha}_j$.

2.5   How Important Are Differences in Economic Performance in the Euro Area?

The discussion so far has concentrated on the theoretical aspects. In this brief section we wish to provide some data on the importance of divergences in economic performance within the euro area. How should one measure the importance of differences in economic performance? The best starting point should be the two loss functions we consider. For the convenience of the reader we recall them briefly.

L^N refers to the case where the union monetary authority (ECB) cares for the weighted average of *national utilities* $L^N \equiv \sum_j \mu_j \lfloor b(n_j)^2 + \pi^2 \rfloor$, where the relative weight of country j (in euro area-wide employment and GDP) is μ_j, with $\sum_j \mu_j = 1$ and the subscript j referring as usual to country j. L^A refers to the case where the ECB bases its decision on an area-wide utility function that uses the *averages of national performances* as input: $L^A \equiv b \lfloor \sum_j \mu_j(n_j) \rfloor^2 + \pi^2$.

Disregarding inflation, which has not been part of our model, we have the result

$$\frac{L^N}{L^A} = \frac{\sum_j \mu_j(n_j)^2}{\lfloor \sum_j \mu_j(n_j) \rfloor^2} \equiv \frac{\text{variance} + (\text{average})^2}{(\text{average})^2}$$

$$\equiv (\text{coefficient of variance})^2 \, C \, 1.$$

This suggests that one could obtain a metric for the importance of divergences in economic performance, and thus for the importance of different decision mechanisms in the ECB as well, by looking at the coefficient of

Table 2.2
Divergences in unemployment in the euro area

Unemployment: euro zone	1997	1998	1999	2000	2001
Weighted (GDP)					
SD	3.7	3.5	3.1	2.7	2.5
Average	11.2	10.6	9.8	8.8	8.2
Covariation	0.33	0.33	0.31	0.31	0.30
Weighted (population)					
SD	4.1	3.8	3.2	2.9	2.6
Average	11.7	11.0	10.1	9.1	8.5
Covariation	0.35	0.34	0.32	0.31	0.30
Nonweighted					
SD	4.8	4.5	4.2	3.8	3.5
Average	9.6	9.0	8.1	7.3	6.8
Covariation	0.49	0.50	0.51	0.53	0.51
Ratio nonweighted SD/weighted SD(GDP)	128	130	136	140	142
Ratio nonweighted SD/weighted SD(population)	117	120	129	133	137

Source: Own calculation based on Eurostat data.
Note: All data for euro-12.

variation of unemployment rates. The data for the euro area over the last years presented in table 2.2 suggests that these differences can be substantial (and that weighting individual country data is crucial).

Table 2.2, in particular, shows that the overall impression conveyed of the importance of differences in growth rates, measured by the standard deviation, depends a lot on whether or not countries are weighed (by their share in euro area GDP or population). The unweighted standard deviations are significantly larger. The simple reason behind this result is that in particular, the smaller countries have rates of unemployment that diverge from those of large countries, i.e., they are often smaller.

2.6   Concluding Remarks

We have found that it makes a difference whether the central bank of a monetary union bases its decisions on the average values of inflation and employment for the entire area, or whether it recognizes that differences in national performance can lead potentially to large differences in national welfare and therefore tries to minimize the average of national welfare. If it minimizes the (weighted) average of national welfare, it will clearly stabilize less than a central bank concerned with unionwide developments would do. It might, on the other hand, also produce a higher inflation bias, however, depending on the relation between the transmission mechanism and the distortions in member countries. Because a central bank that tries to maximize the sum of national welfare levels reacts less to common shocks, the choice of its decision-making mechanism becomes more important as the variance of common shocks increases. We also found that a simply metric can be constructed for the divergences in the euro area, which indicates that they are important.

It is worthwhile to emphasise that our results are completely independent from two issues that usually come up in any discussion of national divergences within EMU. First, whether and how the ECB should weigh the variables from member countries when it calculates area-wide averages (i.e., population or GDP weights). We have assumed that it is appropriate to weight national variables when calculating area averages. The data from the euro area confirm that this is indeed essential, for both calculating averages and intra-area divergences, because otherwise small outliers such as Ireland dominate averages. Table 2.2 shows that indeed, unweighted standard deviations are much higher than the weighted ones. The question of what type of weight is used for calculating the appropriate objective function for the ECB is an important one, but not the issue of this chapter. It actually becomes clear from our analysis that our results are valid independent of any particular weight that is assigned to country j.

A second issue we wanted to avoid was whether different countries have different preferences concerning the trade-off between output and inflation, an issue that much dominated public discussion in countries like Germany. We have explicitly assumed that preferences are the same in all countries, reflecting the evidence that preferences on this seem to have converged over the last decades (Collins and Giavazzi 1993; Hayo 1998).

What is more salient to our study, however, is the question how these objective functions for the central bank, that we have discussed, should be understood and how they can be implemented.

A central bank board that takes simple averages can best be understood as one where there are only true Europeans responsible for monetary policy. This would probably imply that all members of board do only look at European values. This is not very likely to be the case, however. Otherwise, there would be no need for national representatives on the ECB board. Also it would be hard to understand from the political discussion who should be member of the board. Thus it is rather unlikely that we really are in a situation where there is simply averaging going on within the ECB board, despite the fact this is the official rhetoric of the ECB.

The setup where national considerations do have an important role to play in the setting of monetary policy could probably best be understood in reality as a board where national representatives are not only present but explicitly vote in the interest of their own country or region. One might argue if this is the case presently in the ECB. However, our model assumes that this voting takes place according to the relative weight of each country. This, at least, officially is not the case in the ECB, where the one country, one vote principle is the rule. Our model would suggest that this is not the appropriate setup and that from the point of view of this approach countries with a large economic weight should officially (and not only informally) have a higher voting power than smaller ones.

Finally, the whole analysis is driven by the observation that monetary transmission differences do exist. One might argue that EMU will invariably lead to some convergence in the transmission of monetary policy. Therefore one might take the position that our results are not relevant for more than a very short time only. Be that as it may, at present differences exist and the enlargement of EMU will make them even more important. Candidate countries and new members of the EMU will probably have large differences to the present members due to differences in the functioning of labor markets and to different banking systems and industrial structures. Therefore our study will remain relevant in a longer term positive perspective, as it flags some potential problems with enlargement, and in the normative perspective, because it suggests that the problem of how to integrate new members is not just relevant from the point of view of finding an efficient decision-making mechanism.

Notes

We thank conference participants in Munich and one anonymous referee for helpful comments.

1. Rogoff (1985) has argued that independence could be a solution to the problem. He also shows, however, that ultraconservativeness cannot be optimal in a stochastic world.

Thus conservativeness cannot solve the credibility problem entirely, it can only mitigate it. For an overview of the debate, see Hayo and Hefeker (2002).

2. Define $\sum_j \mu_j(\alpha_j - \bar{\alpha})(k_j - \bar{k}) \equiv \theta_{\alpha,k}$, and multiply this out to see that $\sum_j \mu_j \alpha_j k_j = \theta_{\alpha,k} + \bar{\alpha}\bar{k}$.

3. Define $\sum_j \mu_j(\alpha_j - \bar{\alpha})^2 \equiv \theta_\alpha^2$. Multiply out this expression and notice that $-2\sum_j \mu_j \alpha_j \bar{\alpha} + \sum_j \mu_j \bar{\alpha}^2 = -\bar{\alpha}^2$. Thus $\sum_j \mu_j \alpha_j^2 = \theta_\alpha^2 + \bar{\alpha}^2$.

4. Of course, one might speculate about the fact that individual country weights in the setting of monetary policy might be different from their weight according to population or GDP. However, since we have no evidence that this is the case, any speculation about that is just that—speculation.

5. Our theoretical prior would be that α and k are negatively related. However, a simple calculation using data for the transmission mechanism (Cecchetti 1999) and estimates of NAIRUs (taken from Mc Morrow and Roeger 2000) yields a correlation of zero. One explanation for this is that there are obviously more influences on the transmission mechanism than only labor markets.

6. If that were the case, Ω would tend to zero, and the utility difference would tend to zero as well. Thus our discussion implicitly assumes that α_j does not dominate the union values.

References

Alesina, A., and V. Grilli. 1992. The European central bank: Reshaping monetary politics in Europe. In M. Canzoneri, V. Grilli, and P. Masson, eds., *Establishing a Central Bank: Issues in Europe and Lessons from the US*. Cambridge: Cambridge University Press.

Aksoy, Y., P. de Grauwe, and H. Dewachter. 2002. Do asymmetries matter for European monetary policy? *European Economic Review* 46: 443–69.

Angeloni, I., A. Kashayap, B. Mojon, and D. Terlizzese. 2001. Monetary transmission in the euro area: Where do we stand? Mimeo: European Central Bank, Frankfurt.

Barro, R., and D. Gordon. 1983. A positive theory of monetary policy in a natural rate model. *Journal of Political Economy* 91: 589–610.

Blinder, A. 1998. *Central Banking in Theory and Practice*. Cambridge: MIT Press.

Borio, C. 1995. The structure of credit to the non-government sector and the transmission mechanism of monetary policy: A cross-country comparison. Working Paper 24. BIS, Basel.

Cecchetti, S. 1999. Legal structure, financial structure, and the monetary policy transmission mechanism. Federal Reserve Bank of New York, *Economic Policy Review*, July.

Clarida, R., J. Gali, and M. Gertler. 1999. The science of monetary policy: A new Keynesian perspective. *Journal of Economic Literature* 37: 1661–1707.

Collins, S., and F. Giavazzi. 1993. Attitudes towards inflation and the viability of fixed exchange rates. In M. Bordo and B. Eichengreen, eds., *A Retrospective on the Bretton Woods System*. Chicago: University of Chicago Press.

De Grauwe, P. 2000. Monetary policies in the presence of asymmetries. *Journal of Common Market Studies* 38: 593–612.

Eijffinger, S. C. W., and J. de Haan. 2000. *European Monetary and Fiscal Policy*. Oxford: Oxford University Press.

Dornbusch, R., C. Favero, and F. Giavazzi. 1998. Immediate challenges for the European central bank. *Economic Policy* 26: 15–64.

Gerlach, S., and F. Smets. 1995. The monetary transmission mechanism: Evidence from the G-7 countries. Working Paper 26. BIS, Basel.

Gray, J. 1976. Wage indexation: A macroeconomic approach. *Journal of Monetary Economics* 2: 221–35.

Hayo, B. 1998. Inflation culture, central bank independence and price stability. *European Journal of Political Economy* 14: 241–63.

Hayo, B., and C. Hefeker. 2002. Reconsidering central bank independence. *European Journal of Political Economy* 18: 653–74.

Jensen, H. 2001. Explaining an inflation bias without the word "surprise." Mimeo: University of Copenhagen.

Lindbeck, A., and D. Snower. 1988. *The Insider-Outsider Theory of Employment and Unemployment*. Cambridge: MIT Press.

Mc Marrow, K., and W. Roeger. 2000. Time-varying Nairu/Nawru estimates for the EU's member states. Economic Paper 145. EU Commission.

Mihov, I. 2001. Monetary policy implementation and transmission in the European Monetary Union. *Economic Policy* 33: 369–406.

Rudebusch, G. D., and L. E. O. Svensson. 1999. Policy rules for inflation targeting. In J. Taylor, ed., *Monetary Policy Rules*. Chicago: University of Chicago Press.

Svensson, L. E. O. 2001. The inflation forecast and the loss function. Mimeo: Princeton University.

von Hagen, J., and R. Süppel. 1994. Central bank constitutions for federal monetary unions. *European Economic Review* 38: 774–82.

Comment on Chapter 2

Jørgen Elmeskov

This interesting discussion by Gros and Hefeker deals with an issue that we at the OECD have also been confronted with in our *Economic Surveys* of the euro area.[1] The basic premise is that the euro area is different from other currency areas in not being a nation and hence not a political union. Because institutions and nonmonetary policies differ across countries, the effects of a common monetary policy will also differ across countries. And because countries are different, even the same changes in economic performance may well have different welfare effects. The hypothesis of the chapter is that in these conditions, monetary policy should perhaps not maximize an areawide welfare function, defined over areawide averages of economic performance, but rather a weighted average of national welfare functions.

The conclusions of the chapter are that if monetary policy focuses on a weighted average of national welfare functions rather than an aggregate welfare function, then monetary policy

- will tend to stabilize less in the face of areawide shocks, and

- may have more of an inflationary bias.

Gros and Hefeker argue that these results hold

- independently of the choice of weights for aggregating welfare and/ or economic performance, and

- independently of whether preferences differ across countries.

My discussion will focus on these conclusions and some of the model features that produce them. By contrast, I will not discuss the basic hypothesis of the chapter. That should not necessarily be taken as a sign that I agree with it—only that it falls outside the scope of some fairly brief comments. At the end, I will add a few words about the real world.

A model is meant to provide a simplified representation of the real world to allow one to get a grasp of some particular issue. However, some of the simplifications made in the current model to make it more analytically tractable strike me as also making the results less interesting.

One concern is with the assumptions about inflation that seem to stack the cards in favor of the findings in the chapter. The model is first presented in terms of national inflation rates. That is, labor demand depends on national inflation and national welfare depends on national inflation. This would seem to make good descriptive sense. But when the model is then solved, it is assumed that inflation is uniform across the euro area. This short-circuits an important mechanism. The point is that countries that enjoy a particularly steep fall in unemployment usually experience more of an uptick in inflation. In the model, as it is solved, these countries would still benefit from the fall in unemployment but would not have to pay an above-average price in terms of inflation.

With an uneven fall in unemployment rates across countries, the average of national welfares will tend to rise more than the areawide welfare based on average unemployment.[2] The mirror image of this would normally be an uneven rise in inflation across countries, which would reduce the average of national welfares more than the areawide welfare based on average inflation. But this second effect has been shut off in the model by the assumption of a common inflation rate. Against that background it is not surprising that the chapter comes to the conclusion that monetary policy should respond less to a demand impulse in a regime based on maximizing national welfares.

Let me move to the finding that the inflation bias may be higher with a policy geared towards national welfare rather than areawide welfare. As explained in the chapter, it hinges on a particular constellation of parameters in the model. For ease, I reproduce the relevant equations:

$$n_j = \alpha_j \left(\pi_j - \pi_j^e \right) + \varepsilon_j + \varepsilon_{EU} \qquad \text{labor demand}$$

$$L_j = b(n_j - k_j)^2 + \pi_j^2 \qquad \text{loss function}$$

In order to achieve the inflation bias, the covariation across countries has to be positive between the parameter k, which the chapter interprets as a measure of labor market distortions, and the parameter α, which is taken to indicate the effectiveness of monetary policy. The latter is really an indicator of how strongly a demand or inflation surprise affects employment. The chapter is somewhat agnostic on the size and sign of this covariation.

Table 2.3
Covariation between structural unemployment and labor demand responsiveness

Policy	Effect on structural unemployment, k	Effect on employment response to monetary policy, α	Covariation
Employment protection	$(+)$	$-$	$(-)$
Active labor market policy	$-$	$+$	$-$
Unemployment benefits	$+$	$(-)$	$(-)$
Insider bargaining	$+$	$(-)$	$(-)$
Product market composition	$-$	$+$	$-$

In thinking about this result, I find it difficult to interpret the parameter k. The authors clearly think about k as a structural rate of unemployment. But the quadratic loss function is specified in terms of employment deviations from k. This suggests that k is really a structural employment rate or level. That is, k is more an indicator of the absence of distortions than an indicator of their presence. This distinction does not matter much as long as the loss function is quadratic, which goes to show that such a function, while analytically easy to work with, is really not very interesting in a real world context. In any case, when thinking about real life policy implications, it is pretty crucial whether it is k or $1 - k$ that is associated with inflation bias.

My second reaction to the issue of covariation between k and α, and any associated inflation bias, was to think about various policies that affect the labor market and to consider how they would affect the covariation. In doing so, I considered k as representing structural unemployment, which is the way it is described in the chapter (even if that does not seem consistent with the algebra). Thinking about specific policies the following arguments can be made (see table 2.3):

1. Strict employment protection would tend to reduce the response of employment to an unexpected demand shock and would, if anything, tend to put upward pressure on structural unemployment. That is, it would generate a negative correlation.

2. Active labor market policies would tend to put downward pressure on the structural unemployment rate and raise the employment response to an unexpected demand shock. Again, a negative covariation is generated.

3. Generous unemployment benefits raise structural unemployment and, if anything, may reduce the employment response to a demand shock. Again, the covariation is negative.

4. Union wage bargaining governed by insiders is likely to reduce the employment response to a demand shock and to raise structural unemployment. Again, this generates a negative covariation.

5. Strong product market competition is likely to increase the employment responsiveness and to reduce structural unemployment.

After having considered five policy factors commonly associated with structural unemployment, the negative covariations lead by five to nil. However, as shown in the chapter, a positive covariation is needed for the inflation bias to increase with a shift to a policy based on national welfares. All of this depends on k being interpreted as a measure of structural unemployment. If k is really the inverse of what it is presented as in the chapter, then the inflation bias is doing really fine.

A final, minor model-related question relates to the weights used to produce averages. The chapter assumes that the weights to calculate average national welfares are the same as to calculate average employment for use in the areawide welfare function (the authors get around the calculation of an average inflation rate because they assume that inflation is the same in all countries). It is not obvious that one would use the same weights to average welfare as to average employment performance. And if inflation rates had been allowed to differ across countries, then the weights to calculate the average would presumably also have differed. Gros and Hefeker's use of identical weights to average different variables seems to preempt an interesting discussion of what weights to use for calculating averages and weakens the basis for concluding that weights do not matter.

Finally, a few thoughts closer to the real world. What would happen, in practice, if the ECB reacted less to demand shocks and became more tolerant of inflation and defended that with reference to the fact that falls in unemployment in high-unemployment countries may be better for average welfare than falls in low-unemployment countries? A reasonable guess is, nothing good. Monetary policy is not just about doing the right thing but also about getting people to understand that you are doing so. And the communications aspects of following an approach as in the chapter are daunting. As well, being slow to respond to shocks and thereby experiencing bigger and more protracted differences between expected and actual inflation may have some costs in terms of credibility. Besides, following a strategy as outlined in the chapter would make it clearly visible that some countries would lose welfare from a policy that would benefit others.

Summing up, this chapter provides a thought-provoking study. The basic idea is an interesting one. In my comments I have argued that sometimes the simplicity of the model may drive the results, and this suggests an agenda for further research. At the end of the day, however, some of the real world issues related to communications and credibility are hard to model and have a strong influence on the policies actually followed.

Notes

These comments reflect the author's personal view and are not necessarily shared by the OECD or its member governments.

1. See OECD, *EMU: Facts, Challenges and Policies*, Paris, 1999 and OECD, *EMU—One Year On*, Paris, 2000.

2. This result obviously hinges on the shape of welfare functions, as I show next.

3   Is the ECB Too Decentralized?

Jakob de Haan, Helge Berger, and Robert Inklaar

3.1   Introduction

For the first time since the Roman empire, a large portion of Europe shares a common currency since the beginning of 1999. After fifty years the Deutsche Bundesbank—the central bank that ruled European monetary affairs—stepped down to entrust monetary policy to the European Central Bank (ECB). Since the start of the Economic and Monetary Union (EMU) in Europe, the ECB has determined monetary policy in Europe. Like the other ten national central banks in the euro area, the Bundesbank is part of the European System of Central Banks (ESCB).

    The primary objective of the ESCB as prescribed in the Maastricht Treaty is to maintain price stability in the euro zone. The ESCB is governed by the decision-making bodies of the ECB: the Governing Council, the Executive Board, and the General Council (see figure 3.1). The Governing Council of the ECB is the most important decision-making body of the ECB. It consists of the Executive Board of the ECB and the governors of the national central banks of the countries in the euro area. The Executive Board of the ECB consists of the president, the vice president, and up to four other members. The Executive Board implements monetary policy decisions taken by the Governing Council. The main responsibility of the Governing Council is to take decisions in relation to the tasks entrusted to the ESCB. The Governing Council is, for instance, responsible for monetary policy, including decisions about intermediate objectives and interest rates. When taking monetary policy decisions, the members of the Governing Council of the ECB should not act as national representatives, but in a fully independent personal capacity. This is reflected in the principle of "one person, one vote."

    The national central banks of the ESCB are fully engaged in the implementation of policy through the use of their local standing facilities

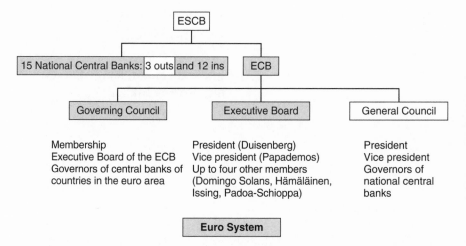

Figure 3.1
Structure of the European system of central banks (December 2002). The General Council
oversees the work of the central banks in various areas, including collection of statistics
and conditions of employment within the ECB. Although the General Council has no role
in setting monetary policy, one of its most important responsibilities is to prepare for an
irrevocable fixing of the exchange rates of the slow track countries. (Source: Eijffinger and
De Haan 2002)

and their participation in open market activities. However, they are
bound by guidelines set by the Governing Council of the ECB.[1] Within
the Governing Council 12 out of the 18 members represent national
central banks. This implies that national central banks have an important say in monetary policy decisions. Due to this voting mechanism
there is a clear difference between the economic size of EMU countries
and their political power.[2]

Table 3.1 compares the ECB with the Federal Reserve and the Bundesbank in terms of economic size of the central banks concerned. It follows that in the United States the regional central banks are of similar
size, whereas in EMU the distribution of economic size is quite uneven.
Note that for at least 7 out of 12 EMU countries their *political* weight
(i.e., 1/18, or about 6 percent of all votes in the Governing Council) exceeds their *economic* weight (i.e., 0–5 percent of EMU GDP).[3] Germany
is in-between: the central banks of Nordrhein-Westfalen (22 percent)
and Bavaria (17 percent) have substantially more economic power than
most of the other banks. Table 3.2 compares the ECB with the German
and American central banks in terms of the power of the regional central banks. Also from this perspective, the decision-making structure of

Table 3.1
Share in total GDP of central banks (distribution), 1999

Share in GDP (%)	Germany[a]	United States	EMU
0–5	0	1	7
5–10	5	10	2
10–15	2	0	0
15–20	1	1	1
20–30	1	0	1
>30	0	0	1
Total	9	12	12

Source: Fase and Vanthoor (2000) and own calculations.
a. Germany: 1998.

Table 3.2
Distribution of voting power: Center and regions

Bank	Center	Regions	Center/region
Buba before 1957	1	9	0.11
Buba before 1992	7	11	0.64
Buba before 1999	8	9	0.89
FED	7	5	1.40
ECB 1999	6	11	0.55
ECB 2001	6	12	0.50

Source: Own calculations.

ECB is quite different from those of comparable central banks. The national central banks have a very important say in European monetary policy making.

An important question is whether this institutional setup could lead to conflicts. If, for instance, inflation in Germany and France—most of the euro zone—is in line with the objective of price stability while in some small countries inflation is increasing, will the governors of the central banks of the latter countries favor a reduction in interest rates? Of course, the ECB may also be to reluctant to reduce interest rates. For instance, Sinn (2001, p. 2) argues: "The European Central Bank's failure to lower interest rates at its last meeting, although US rates are now below those in Europe, was very disappointing. Is the boom in Ireland and Finland so important for Europe that it prevents battling recession in the heart of the Continent? Where is the much-touted responsibility of every individual member of the Central Bank for the whole, for the sake of which Germany contented itself with only half of the voting strength of these two countries even though it is nine times as large?"

Crucial here is to what extent inflation differentials and differences in business cycles exist in EMU and whether they will remain. But even if inflation and business cycles were very similar, there could be conflicts in the ECB Governing Council due to differences in preferences.

The remainder of this chapter is organized as follows. Section 3.2 presents a very simple model broadly following De Grauwe (2000b). Section 3.3 focuses on the German experience, while section 3.4 analyzes business cycles asymmetries in the EMU countries. Section 3.5 goes into differences in preferences in the euro zone. A final section goes into the policy conclusions.

3.2   A Simple Model

The model presented in this section is a variant of the model of De Grauwe (2000b).[4] We first assume that the monetary union consists of two countries: R and F and that the monetary authority in the monetary union has the following loss function:

$$L_E = \gamma L_R + (1 - \gamma)L_F,$$ (3.1)

where L_R and L_F are the loss functions of the countries R and F and γ is the share of country R. The parameter γ can be interpreted as the weight given to country R in the *political* decision process. In other words, we first assume that monetary policy is a weighted function of the loss functions of the individual countries. A possible perspective on (3.1) is that individual representatives of the countries in the ECB Governing Council aim to influence monetary policy in the direction of their *national* policy targets as embedded in their respective loss functions. While clearly not in line with the objectives laid down in the formal ECB framework (see below), this scenario might well be a good description of the actual behavior of Governing Council members. The loss function of each individual country is written as

$$L_R = \pi^2 + b_R(Y_R - Y_R^*)^2,$$ (3.2)

$$L_F = \pi^2 + b_F(Y_F - Y_F^*)^2,$$ (3.3)

where π is the common inflation rate, Y_R and Y_F are output in countries R and F and $(Y_R - Y_R^*)$ and $(Y_F - Y_F^*)$ are the output gaps that the authorities wish to minimize; b denotes the weight given to output stabilization. The ratio $1/b$ is often interpreted as a measure of "conservativeness" (i.e., inflation aversion). Output in the two countries is determined according to the Lucas supply curve

$$Y_R = Y_R^* - \alpha(\pi - \pi^e) + \varepsilon_R, \tag{3.4}$$

$$Y_F = Y_F^* - \alpha(\pi - \pi^e) + \varepsilon_F, \tag{3.5}$$

where ε_R and ε_F represent stochastic disturbances with mean 0 and known variance in the two countries. Inflation π is, for simplicity purposes only, interpreted as a policy instrument. We assume that transmission of monetary impulses, namely the differences between π and expected inflation π^e, in the two countries is the same (see De Grauwe 2000b for the analysis with differences in transmission). Thus asymmetries can appear in two forms in this model. One is an asymmetry in the disturbances ($\varepsilon_R \neq \varepsilon_F$), the other is an asymmetry in preferences ($b_R \neq b_F$).

To determine the optimal inflation rate, substitute equation (3.4) in (3.2) and equation (3.5) in (3.3). Then substitute both equations in (3.1) and minimize this function with respect to π. Under rational expectations inflation will then be

$$\pi|_{(1)} = \frac{\alpha\gamma b_R \varepsilon_R + \alpha(1-\gamma)b_F \varepsilon_F}{1 + \alpha^2(\gamma b_R + (1-\gamma)b_F)}, \tag{3.6}$$

where the index (1) marks the case in which inflation in the euro zone is set in line with the loss function described in equation (3.1).

Alternatively, assume that the monetary authority in the monetary union has the following loss function

$$L_E = \pi^2 + b_E \langle \lambda(Y_R - Y_R^*) + (1-\lambda)(Y_F - Y_F^*) \rangle^2, \tag{3.7}$$

where λ denotes the *economic* weight of country R. This situation is more or less what the architects of the ECB system had in mind when specifying the normative standards that *should* be guiding monetary policy in the euro zone. After all, the primary objective of all Council members should be price stability in the euro area as a whole and not the implied welfare in an individual country as in loss function (3.1). Instead, loss function (3.7) implies that the ECB minimizes deviations of euro zone averages of inflation and output from their targets. Consequently the effective weight given to an individual country in the underlying policy decision process is defined by its economic size λ rather than its political weight as in (3.1). Using (3.7), but otherwise following the same steps as above, we find that

$$\pi|_{(7)} = \frac{\alpha b_E(\lambda \varepsilon_R + (1-\lambda)\varepsilon_F)}{1+\alpha^2 b_E}. \tag{3.8}$$

The index (7) marks the scenario in which monetary policy is found based on loss function (3.7).

To evaluate the effect of asymmetric shocks, different preferences and the two loss functions, we calculate the expected variance of the loss function of each country

$$E(L_R) = \operatorname{var} \pi^2 + b_R \operatorname{var} Y_R^2, \tag{3.9}$$

where we have assumed that Y_R^* is constant. Calculating the variance of (3.6) yields

$$\operatorname{var} \pi|_{(1)} = \left(\frac{\alpha}{1+\alpha^2(\gamma b_R + (1-\gamma)b_F)}\right)^2 (\gamma^2 b_R^2 \operatorname{var} \varepsilon_R$$

$$+ (1-\gamma)^2 b_F^2 \operatorname{var} \varepsilon_F + 2(\gamma - \gamma^2)b_R b_F \operatorname{cov} \varepsilon_R \varepsilon_F), \tag{3.10}$$

while the variance of (3.8) is

$$\operatorname{var} \pi|_{(7)} = \left(\frac{\alpha b_E}{1+\alpha^2 b_E}\right)^2 (\lambda^2 \operatorname{var} \varepsilon_R + (1-\lambda)^2 \operatorname{var} \varepsilon_F$$

$$+ 2(\lambda - \lambda^2) \operatorname{cov} \varepsilon_R \varepsilon_F). \tag{3.11}$$

In (3.10) and (3.11) the effects of *asymmetric shocks* are clear. If the covariance between ε_R and ε_F is large, inflation will have a larger variance. Put differently, if both countries are hit by symmetric shocks, the monetary authorities can stabilize output in both economies simultaneously by increasing inflation. If the shocks are largely asymmetric, monetary authorities will not be able to react effectively to either shock.

So what is the effect of differences in the *political and economic weight* of a country? To simplify, assume that $b_R = b_F = b_E$, namely that there are no differences in preferences between countries R and F. In this case (3.10) would change to

$$\operatorname{var} \pi|_{(1)} = \left(\frac{\alpha b_E}{1+\alpha^2 b_E}\right)^2 (\gamma^2 \operatorname{var} \varepsilon_R + (1-\gamma)^2 \operatorname{var} \varepsilon_F$$

$$+ 2(\gamma - \gamma^2) \operatorname{cov} \varepsilon_R \varepsilon_F). \tag{3.10a}$$

Obviously, then, from the perspective of country R, the variance of inflation would be higher in regime (3.1) if $\gamma > \lambda$. This follows straight from a comparison of (3.10a) and (3.11). Note, however, that this implies a welfare gain rather than a welfare loss from the perspective of country R. Indeed, for $\gamma \to 1 > \lambda$ the euro zone's monetary policy under regime (3.1) approaches country R's first best response to shocks ε_R.[5] Consequently, if the political weight of a country is larger than its economic weight, it is more likely to prefer a monetary policy regime based on (3.1).

Yet another perspective we can introduce is to look at the differences in *preferences*. To shed light on this issue, assume that countries are similar in political and economic size, namely $\gamma = \lambda = 1/2$. Under this symmetry assumption we can rewrite equations (3.10) and (3.11) as

$$\text{var } \pi|_{(1)} = \left(\frac{\alpha}{1 + \alpha^2(b_R + b_F)/2} \right)^2 \frac{1}{4} \left(b_R^2 \text{ var } \varepsilon_R + b_F^2 \text{ var } \varepsilon_F \right) \qquad (3.10b)$$

and

$$\text{var } \pi|_{(7)} = \left(\frac{\alpha}{1 + \alpha^2 b_E} \right)^2 \frac{1}{4} \left(b_E^2 \text{ var } \varepsilon_R + b_E^2 \text{ var } \varepsilon_F \right). \qquad (3.11a)$$

A comparison of equations (3.10b) and (3.11a) reveals that unless the output preference governing monetary policy under regime (3.7) b_E is identical to country R's preference b_R country R is likely to be further away from its desired outcome under regime (3.7) than under regime (3.1). This will always be the case if, for instance, the foreign loss function shares the "conservative" output preference with the ECB, that is, if $b_F = b_E < b_R$.

How will these differences in monetary policy under both regimes influence output? In general, the variance of output is

$$\text{var } Y_R = \text{var}(\varepsilon_R - \alpha\pi) = \alpha^2 \text{ var } \pi + \text{var } \varepsilon_R - 2 \text{ cov } \varepsilon_R \pi, \qquad (3.12)$$

as both the natural output Y^* and the expected inflation π^e are fixed variables. Since we have already described the characteristics of the variance of inflation, we can restrict ourselves to discussing the covariance between the countries' shocks and inflation. This covariance will determine the extent to which the common monetary policy in the euro zone will stabilize a country's economy. Since the model is symmetric in this respect, we can focus on country R without loss of generality. We find that

$$\text{cov } \varepsilon_R \pi|_{(1)} = \frac{\alpha}{1 + \alpha^2(\gamma b_R + (1 - \gamma)b_F)}$$

$$\cdot (\gamma b_R \text{ var } \varepsilon_R + (1 - \gamma)b_F \text{ cov } \varepsilon_R \varepsilon_F), \qquad (3.13)$$

$$\text{cov } \varepsilon_R \pi|_{(7)} = \frac{\alpha b_E}{1 + \alpha^2 b_E}(\lambda \text{ var } \varepsilon_R + (1 - \lambda) \text{ cov } \varepsilon_R \varepsilon_F). \qquad (3.14)$$

Equation (3.13) is the covariance for inflation given by (3.6) implied by regime (3.1), while equation (3.14) is the covariance for inflation given by (3.8) implied by regime (3.7). Both results show that the covariance will be higher if the *shocks* in both countries are highly correlated (a result also found by De Grauwe 2000b).

Furthermore, an increased *weight* in the monetary policy decision process, given by a higher γ, or a higher λ, also results in a higher covariance. More important, countries that are endowed with a larger political than economic influence will, in general, favor a monetary policy regime characterized by equation (3.1). To illustrate, assume again that $b_R = b_F = b_E$. Then (3.13) can be rewritten as

$$\text{cov } \varepsilon_R \pi|_{(1)} = \frac{\alpha b_E}{1 + \alpha^2 b_E}(\gamma \text{ var } \varepsilon_R + (1 - \gamma) \text{ cov } \varepsilon_R \varepsilon_F). \qquad (3.13a)$$

Comparing (3.13a) with (3.14) it can be seen that countries with $\gamma > \lambda$ will enjoy a higher covariance of ε_R and π and thus a lower variance of output under policy regime (3.1) than under regime (3.7). Since, as argued above, the increase in inflation variance will be optimal in the sense that the welfare gain from lower output volatility dominates the welfare loss from more volatile inflation, in this example, countries with $\gamma > \lambda$ will also enjoy higher welfare in regime (3.1) than (3.7).

Similarly, following the discussion on *preferences* above, we can also state that under symmetry in weights, namely $\gamma = \lambda = 1/2$, (3.13) and (3.14) become

$$\text{cov } \varepsilon_R \pi|_{(1)} = \frac{\alpha}{1 + \alpha^2(\gamma b_R + (1 - \gamma)b_F)}\frac{1}{2}(b_R \text{ var } \varepsilon_R + b_F \text{ cov } \varepsilon_R \varepsilon_F),$$

$$(3.13b)$$

$$\text{cov } \varepsilon_R \pi|_{(7)} = \frac{\alpha b_E}{1 + \alpha^2 b_E}\frac{1}{2}(\text{var } \varepsilon_R + \text{ cov } \varepsilon_R \varepsilon_F). \qquad (3.14a)$$

Using the example introduced above, if $b_F = b_E < b_R$, that is, if the foreign loss function shares the conservative output preference of the ECB, then the covariance under regime (3.1) is unambiguously larger (and output variance lower) than under regime (3.7).

There are two basic messages to be drawn from this theoretical exercise. First, the common monetary policy will be more active (and output volatility will be lower) if country *shocks* are highly correlated. The reason is that if the covariance between ε_R and ε_F is positive and high, a strong reaction of the euro zone's stabilization policy to an output shock in a particular country will be more or less in line with the stabilization needs of other members of the euro area. In that sense, the ECB could be "too decentralized" if business cycle synchronicity in the euro zone would be low or not converging.

Second, the distribution of political preferences and the asymmetry between *political and economic weights* of euro zone member countries in the decision-making process could have an important influence on their behavior in the Governing Council. If the political weight (or voting power) a given country enjoys in the Council is larger than its economic weight (as applied in the computation of, say, euro zone inflation or rate of output growth), a country's welfare is larger in a regime in which the ECB decision process maximizes the weighted sum of national welfare functions rather than following the norms laid down in the ECB status. Interestingly, as we showed in section 3.1, the political power of the majority of member countries in the euro area exceeds their economic size. Consequently, if the representatives of these politically "overrepresented" countries in the ECB Governing Council let their national welfare perspective govern their behavior in the decision-making process, the ECB might not behave in line with its statute. In fact the ECB might behave as if implementing a political equilibrium based on voting power rather than maximizing the welfare of the euro zone as measured by the deviation of area-wide economic aggregates. Since the political weight of individual members is a function of the strength of national central bank representatives relative to the centralized appointed members of the Executive Board, the ECB might be "too decentralized."

A similar conclusion might be drawn from the occurrence of *political differences* among national central bank representatives. A possible scenario is, for instance, that a majority of representatives has less conservative preferences on the inflation–output-volatility trade-off than what the ECB statute demands.[6] Then, again, the aforementioned asymmetry between political and economic clout could cause the ECB to behave as if being governed by a political equilibrium determined by national interests rather than following the targets specified in its status.

What would be the *policy implications* of a "too decentralized" monetary policy in the euro zone? There is certainly no quick fix to the observed asymmetry between the political and economic weights of ECB member countries. One obvious solution would be to strengthen the voting power of the Executive Board. This could help to mitigate incentives to translate differences in economic development and policy preferences into undesired ECB behavior based on a national rather than a unified euro zone perspective. Section 3.6 will further discuss implications of a "too decentralized" ECB policy. But first we have to ask just *how relevant* is the overall issue empirically. For instance, how important or persistent are the problems of nonsynchronized business cycles in the euro zone today? And is there evidence that a lack of such synchronicity will actually translate into a national-centered behavior of Council members? Is there actually a problem of diverging degrees of conservativeness among the representatives of the national central banks in the ECB? In what follows we will shed some light on these and other questions.

3.3   The German Experience

As the model in the previous section has shown, diverging economic developments may induce national central bankers to dissent. The German experience with a federal central bank structure may be relevant to examining how likely is such an outcome. Like the ECB, the Bundesbank is widely perceived as taking price stability as its primary objective. If we can find evidence that nevertheless economic differences across states influenced Bundesbank policies, we may likewise worry about ECB policies. We first analyze economic developments in the various states and then present some results on voting in the Zentralbankrat, namely the Governing Council of the Bundesbank.

3.3.1   Inflation and Business Cycles in the German States
It is interesting for at least two reasons to analyze differences in economic developments in the German states. First, there is a debate whether over time economic and monetary integration will lead to

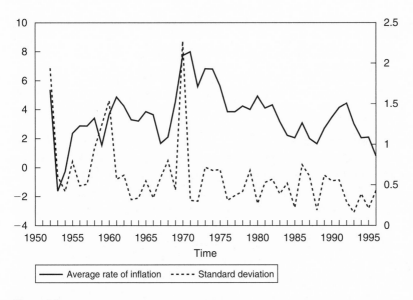

Figure 3.2
Inflation in the German states, 1950 to 1996.

more synchronized business cycles (see section 3.4 for further details).
If integration leads to synchronization of business cycles, the cyclical
patterns of the various German states should have become more similar over time. Second, if there are substantial differences among the
economic developments in the various states, we may analyze whether
these differences have affected the behavior of the presidents of the
Landeszentralbanken, the representatives of "national" (regional state)
central banks in the Governing Council of the Bundesbank.

We start with inflation differentials in the German states. Our sample
period is 1950 to 1996.[7] Figure 3.2 shows that except for some spikes,
the standard deviation of the inflation rates across the German states
has remained fairly constant over time. In other words, there were substantial inflation differentials between the various states.

To analyze the issue of business cycle synchronization, we have followed the methodology of Artis and Zhang (1997, 1999). Using annual
data on real gross state product, we calculated a cyclical index for each
series, which takes the following form:

$$1 + \frac{(X_t - \text{trend}_t)}{\text{trend}_t}, \tag{3.15}$$

where X_t is the raw series and trend$_t$ is the detrended series. Following Artis and Zhang, we employed the Hodrick-Prescott filter (HP filter, with a λ of 100) to determine the trend. This filter is

$$\min_{g_t} \left[\sum_{t=1}^{N}(y_t - g_t)^2 + \lambda \sum_{t=2}^{N-1}[(g_{t+1} - g_t) - (g_t - g_{t-1})]^2 \right]. \qquad (3.16)$$

In this formula y_t represents the series and g_t the growth component. The first part is the cyclical component and the second part the trend. When λ goes to infinity, the formula converges to a linear trend. To analyze whether business cycles in the German states have synchronized over time, we followed two approaches. First, figure 3.3 shows the standard deviation of the cyclical components for each year of our sample period. It clearly follows that business cycles have become more similar in the German states over time. Second, we calculated the cyclical index for each state and computed the correlation between each state's index and the German index, excluding the state concerned. Table 3.3 shows the results, focusing on four subperiods. As before, there is clear evidence that over time business cycles have become more synchronized in Germany. Nevertheless, during each period the economic situation in some states was out of line with the rest. For instance, during the period 1950 to 1960

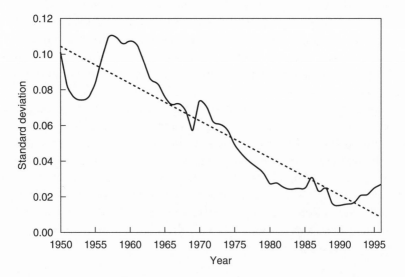

Figure 3.3
Standard deviation of cyclical components in German states, 1950 to 1996.

Table 3.3
Correlation of cyclical index of states with cyclical index of Germany

	1950–1960	1961–1973	1974–1985	1986–1996
Baden-Württemberg	0.16	0.28	0.29	0.92
Bavaria	0.13	0.82	0.76	0.30
Bremen	0.51	0.18	0.40	0.63
Hamburg	0.85	0.96	0.98	0.99
Hesse	0.76	0.90	0.93	0.94
Lower Saxonia	0.67	0.91	0.72	0.96
Nordrhein-Westphalen	0.94	0.98	0.98	0.98
Rheinland-Pfalz	0.62	0.97	0.99	0.99
Schleswig-Hollstein	0.84	0.98	0.97	0.94
Average	0.61	0.78	0.78	0.85

the economies of Baden-Württemberg and Bavaria clearly diverged from those of most other states. As we have information on voting in the governing council of the Bundesbank, we can test whether these differences have affected the behavior of the presidents of the various central banks.

3.3.2 Voting Behavior in the Zentralbankrat, 1948–1961

We have data on individual voting behavior on discount rate changes in the period 1948 to 1961 as reported in Berger (1997, app.).[8] The discount rate is the interest rate charged by the central bank for refinancing through the discount window—by far the most important source of bank refinancing at the time. The discount rate is widely viewed as an excellent indicator for the German central bank's monetary policy stance during the 1950s and 1960s. As a rule other policy instruments (minimum reserve requirements, open market activities, etc.) moved in line with changes of the discount rate. The data are not without problems, though. Actual voting records are not always complete, and some results had to be meticulously gathered from Council discussions. Another caveat is that voting results are available only for *actual* policy decisions and almost no information is available about votes on decisions *not* to change policy.

All in all, there are 180 observations available on voting by nine regional representatives in the governing council, namely the presidents of the local *Landeszentralbanken:* Bavaria (BY), Bremen (HB), Hamburg (HH), Hesse (HS), Lower Saxony (NS), Nordrhein-Westfalen (NRW),

Table 3.4
Dissenting voting behavior in the central bank

Variable	Coefficient	Standard error	z-Statistic	Probability
Constant	−1.865	0.602	−3.099	0.002
D_INF^2	0.122	0.051	2.374	0.018
D_GROWTH^2	−0.050	0.033	−1.505	0.132
(D_DISKONT/	10.581	3.831	2.762	0.006
DISKONT)^2				
BY	0.698	0.632	1.105	0.269
HB	0.259	0.693	0.373	0.709
HH	0.438	0.617	0.709	0.478
HS	1.312	0.625	2.098	0.036
NS	−0.154	0.753	−0.204	0.838
NRW	0.757	0.611	1.239	0.215
RP	0.446	0.591	0.754	0.451
BW	0.267	0.662	0.403	0.687
Mean dependent variable	0.161	SD dependent variable		0.369
LR statistic (11 df)	25.25	McFadden R-squared		0.159
Akaike info criterion	0.88	Schwarz criterion		1.09
Probability(LR stat)	0.008	Number of observations		180

Note: Dependent variable: DISVO.

Rheinland-Pfalz (RP), Baden-Württemberg (BW), and Schleswig-Holstein (SH). There are 151 "yes" votes and 29 "no" or "abstain" votes in the sample.

We first analyzed whether the probability to deviate from a majority vote on a discount rate change was influenced by regional economic developments. Table 3.4 reports results of a pooled ML probit regression of DISVO, a binary variable that is 1 if a regional representative did *not vote "yes"* on a discount rate change favored by the majority of votes in the Council, and 0 otherwise, on a number of explanatory variables. D_INF^2 is the squared deviation of regional inflation from the inflation average of the nine regions contained in the sample. D_GROWTH^2 is the squared deviation of regional real GDP growth from the sample average. (D_DISKONT/DISKONT)^2 is the squared change of the discount rate weighted by the pre-change level of the rate. BY, . . . , BW are regional dummies (the dummy for SH has been omitted).

The results are to be interpreted carefully as the sample by its very nature is somewhat unbalanced. Still, the results suggest that regional differences do indeed play a role in dissent voting. In particular, our findings indicate that the probability of dissent voting significantly increases in the *size of the policy change*. This is not surprising, as one would expect opinions in the Council to deviate more when greater policy changes were contemplated. Furthermore there is some impact of *differences between regional and average real growth*. It would seem that such differences lowered the probability to cast a dissent vote. Note, however, that the estimated coefficient is only significant at the 13 percent level. At the same time the probability of a regional representative not to vote "yes" on a policy change was significantly larger the larger were the *differences between regional and average inflation*. The coefficient is significant at the 5 percent level.[9] The quantitative impact of two of the three variables on DISVO is at least notable. Evaluated at sample means, a one-standard deviation increase in the growth difference (in the inflation difference) increases the probability of casting a dissent vote by 0.75 (by 0.44). Based on the same criterion the impact size of the policy change is an order of magnitude smaller (0.01).

In what follows, we will try to evaluate the direction of dissent voting in more detail. To evaluate the *direction* of dissent voting by regional representatives in the Council, we constructed the hypothetical time path of the preferred discount rates, $r_{i,t}^*$, for every region i at time t. Time refers to the time of actual discount rate decisions. The preferred rate is defined as

$$r_{i,t}^* = r_{i,t-1}^* + (1 - \text{DISVO}_t) \cdot \text{D\_DISKONT}_t; \qquad (3.17)$$

that is, $r_{i,t}^*$ is the discount rate that *would have prevailed*, had only discount rate changes (D_DISKONT) been allowed that region i approved by voting "yes" in the Council (DISVO = 1) at time t. The starting value of $r_{i,t}^*$ at time $t = 0$ has been set to the actual discount rate in the first sample period for all regions. We then regressed the deviation of the preferred discount rate to the actual discount rate, r_t, on the deviation of regional inflation from the inflation average of the nine regions contained in the sample (D_INF) and the deviation of regional real GDP growth from the sample average (D_GROWTH). The estimated panel OLS-model also allows for fixed effects and region-specific time trends (not reported in table 3.5):

$$r_{i,t}^* - r_t = \alpha_i + \beta_i \cdot \text{TREND} + \gamma \cdot \text{D\_INF}_i + \delta \cdot \text{D\_GROWTH}_i + u_{i,t}.$$

$$(3.18)$$

We find that the difference between a region's preferred discount rate and the actual discount rate was a positive function of the *differences between regional and average inflation*. That is, a region with above-average

Table 3.5
Direction of dissent voting in the central bank

Variable	Coefficient	Standard error	t-Statistic	Probability
D_INFi	0.077	0.042	1.847	0.067
D_GROWTHi	−0.055	0.019	−2.982	0.003
R-squared	0.943	Mean dependent variable		−1.435
Adjusted R-squared	0.937	SD dependent variable		1.657
SE of regression	0.417	Sum-squared residual		27.805
Log likelihood	91.646	F-Statistic		266.93
Number of observations	180	Prob(F-statistic)		0.00

Note: Dependent variable: $r_{i,t}^* - r_t$. White heteroskedasticity-consistent standard errors and covariance. Fixed effects and region-specific time trends not reported.

rates of inflation, as a rule, would have preferred a higher discount rate than the Council majority (7 percent significance level). At the same time the difference between a region's preferred and actual discount rate was a negative function of the *differences between regional and average real growth* (1 percent level of significance). This seems to imply that, while above-average inflation caused regions to be relatively "hawkish" judged by their preferred discount rate, they turned into "doves" relative to the Council majority when it came to real growth. This is probably best interpreted as evidence that regions with above-average growth rates hoped to extent their relative prosperity unless this growth experience caused relative inflation to rise too.

In related work Berger and Woitek (1999) have shown that dissent voting in the early Bundesbank Council was also correlated with *political preferences*. Following Vaubel (1997), they categorize Council members according to the political color of their nominating state or federal government.[10] Using the same data set as above, they report that left-wing Council members nominated by social-democratic governments showed a significant tendency to resist (or not to support) interest rate increases. Moreover Berger and Woitek (1999) also report a systematic influence of the degree of conservatism in the Bundesbank Council on German monetary policy in 1950 to 1994. As a rule more conservative Bundesbank Councils (i.e., Councils with a majority of members appointed by conservative governments) tended to be more "active" in their reaction to both output (or demand) and inflation (or supply) shocks.[11] We conclude that the German experience suggests that not only divergence in regional economic development but also differences in political preferences seem to influence actual central bank behavior.

3.4 Diverging Economic Developments in EMU?

To what extent do business cycles in the euro zone differ so that they may hamper a common monetary policy? No matter how important differences in business cycles have been in the past, the crucial question in the present context is how likely they are to remain in the future. Two views have been put forward on this issue. According to a study by the European Commission (Emerson et al. 1992), further economic and monetary integration will lead to less divergence. However, Krugman (1991) poses the opposite. He argues that trade integration will lead to regional concentration of industrial activities. In Europe a similar concentration of industries will take place as in the United States (e.g., Silicon Valley). This concentration process is caused by economies of scale. Due to this concentration process, sector-specific shocks may become region-specific shocks, thereby increasing the likelihood of divergence. Figure 3.4 summarizes both views (De Grauwe 2000).

Which view is correct? The discussion of the German experience in the previous section as well as some recent research provides support for the view that more economic and monetary integration will lead to less divergence. For instance, Frankel and Rose (1998) find that the more countries trade, the more business cycles in these countries are synchronized. Similar results are reported by Artis and Zhang (1997, 1999) and Fatás (1997) who analyze the influence of monetary integration. They find that over time countries participating in the ERM show a strong synchronization of business cycles, in contrast to countries that do not participate. In other words, it follows from these studies that if EMU furthers integration, the likelihood of asymmetric shocks will diminish.

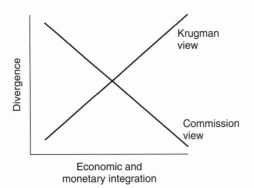

Figure 3.4
Two views on the relationship between economic and monetary integration and divergence.

However, other studies find opposite results for the impact on monetary integration on business cycle synchronization. Frankel and Rose (1998) included a dummy variable, which is one when two countries have linked their currencies, and zero otherwise, and found that its coefficient is not significant. Also Baxter and Stockman (1989) and Inklaar and De Haan (2001) report no effect of the exchange rate on business cycle synchronization.

In the remainder of this section we analyze to what extent business cycle synchronization in the OECD area has been affected by trade intensity and exchange rate volatility. Our sample includes observations for 18 OECD countries over the years 1961 to 1997.[12] The monthly industrial production figures that we used are from the International Financial Statistics of the IMF. To calculate the *correlation* between business cycles we first de-trended the series with a Hodrick-Prescott filter (as we now have monthly data, λ is set to 50,000) and calculated the cyclical indicators in the same way as in the previous section. To avoid mixing periods of differing exchange rate regimes, we divided our sample into the four phases:

1961–1973   In most of this period the Bretton-Woods system was still in place

1973–1979   A period without stable exchange rate arrangement within Europe

1979–1987   The first ERM period with gradually stabilizing exchange rates

1987–1997   The second ERM period almost without realignments

The various subperiods are more or less homogeneous with regard to exchange rate stability. Moreover each of these periods covers an entire business cycle. We estimated the following simple model:

$$\rho_{ij,t} = \alpha_{0,t} + \alpha_1 wt_{ij,t} + \alpha_2 v_{ij,t} + \mu_{ij,t}, \tag{3.19}$$

where $\rho_{ij,t}$ denotes the correlation of the business cycles of countries i and j during the period t, $w_{ij,t}$ denotes our measure for trade intensity during period t, and $v_{ij,t}$ is our measure for exchange rate volatility during period t. Our definition of *trade intensity* is the same as in Frankel and Rose (1998):

$$wt_{ij,t} = \frac{X_{ij,t} + M_{ij,t}}{X_{i,t} + X_{j,t} + M_{i,t} + M_{j,t}}, \tag{3.20}$$

Table 3.6
OLS estimates of the relationship between business cycle correlation and trade and exchange rate volatility

	(1)	(2)	(3)
Constant	44.4	44.6	68.7
	(8.45)	(4.28)	(5.33)
Dummy 1960–73	−12.3	−10.0	−7.6
	(−3.24)	(−2.48)	(−1.85)
Dummy 1973–79	17.2	16.7	16.9
	(4.02)	(3.95)	(3.97)
Dummy 1979–87	0.8	0.6	0.9
	(0.25)	(0.18)	(0.26)
Log(trade intensity)	2.51		3.03
	(2.51)		(2.87)
Log(exchange rate volatility)		2.52	4.50
		(1.23)	(2.15)

Notes: Dependent variable: $\rho_{ij,t}$. t-statistic in parentheses, $n = 612$; all parameters are multiplied by 100.

or the total trade (export plus import) between countries i and j divided by the sum of the trade of each country. The trade data are from the OECD ITCS publication. For the *exchange rate volatility*, we took the standard deviation over a time period of the following expression:

$$v_{ij,t} = \log \left(\frac{E_{ij,t}}{E_{ij,t-1}} \right). \tag{3.21}$$

In this expression $E_{ij,t}$ is the exchange rate between countries i and j at time t.

The results of simple OLS regressions for the entire sample of 612 observations[13] are shown in table 3.6. It follows that higher trade intensity leads to more synchronization of business cycles. This result confirms the findings of Frankel and Rose (1998). Very remarkable, however, is the positive (and sometimes) significant coefficient for exchange rate volatility. This indicates that more exchange rate stability leads to less business cycle synchronization. In other words, our results suggest that further monetary integration will lead to more diverging business cycles.

3.5   Different Preferences in the Euro Zone?

Although the relative inflation aversion ("conservativeness") plays a crucial role in the theoretical literature on monetary policy (see Berger et al. 2001 for a survey), there is only scant empirical evidence on this

Table 3.7
Conservativeness as embodied in the central bank laws during the 1980s

Country	GMT index[a]	Cukierman index[b]
Austria	1	0.60
Belgium/Luxembourg	0	0.00
Finland	na	0.80
France	0	0.00
Germany	1	1.00
Greece	0	0.80
Ireland	1	0.80
Italy	0	0.20
Netherlands	1	0.80
Portugal	0	na
Spain	0	0.60

Source: De Haan and Kooi (1997).
a. Score is one (monetary stability is among the goals of the central bank), or zero.
b. Scores range from zero (stated objectives for central bank do not include price stability) to one (price stability is the only objective).

issue. Various approaches have been suggested in the literature to come up with empirical proxies for the preferences of monetary policy makers.[14] First, whether the statute of a central bank defines price stability as the primary policy goal can be considered as a proxy for the "conservative bias" of the central bank as embodied in the law (Cukierman 1992). Following this line of reasoning, De Haan and Kooi (1997) and Kilponen (1999) have decomposed indicators of central bank independence, which are based on central bank laws during the 1980s, into an indicator for the conservativeness of the central bank as embodied in the law and an indicator for independence proper. Table 3.7 shows the outcomes. It follows that the laws of the central banks in the countries that are currently in the euro zone differed substantially as far as the objectives of monetary policy is concerned.

As already discussed, Berger and Woitek (1999) follow a very different approach. They find that German monetary policy was significantly influenced by the political preferences of its members. As a rule members of the Governing Council of the Bundesbank appointed by governments dominated by the conservative party were more "inflation-averse"— in the sense that they, for instance, reacted more aggressively to inflation shocks—than those nominated by governments dominated by

Table 3.8
Governors of national central banks and their political background

Country	Governor	Political background	Government responsible for appointment
Austria	K. Liebscher	C	S+C
Belgium	G. Quaden	S	L+S+
Finland	M. Vanhala	C	S+C+L
France	J.-C. Trichet	C	C
Germany	E. Welteke	S	S+
Greece	L. D. Papademos	S	S
Ireland	M. O'Connell	?	C
Italy	A. Fazio	C	S+C
Luxembourg	Y. Mersch	C	C+L
Netherlands	N. Wellink	C	S+L
Portugal	V. M. Ribeiro Constâncio	S	S
Spain	V. Caruana	S	C

Source: ECB homepage, Vaubel (1999).
Note: S: socialist or social democratic; C: conservative or Christian democratic; L: liberal.

social-democrats (see section 3.3.2). Something similar is demonstrated by table 3.8, which lists the current presidents of the various national central banks in the EU, their political background, and the "political color" of the government that appointed them.

While the available indicators are certainly not without problems, we conclude that there still seem to be ample differences in the degree of conservativeness in the euro zone. An open question remains whether these differences in preferences are in decline, namely whether there is convergence in preferences comparable to the convergence in business cycle movements described earlier. Perhaps a glance on the answer can be caught by turning to the time path of certain macroeconomic variables. Thus our final empirical investigation focuses on inflation and on the volatility of output. Figure 3.5 shows inflation while figure 3.6 shows the standard deviation of real output growth.

As is clear from figure 3.5 euro zone member countries, despite some variance across time and countries, shared a common trend toward lower inflation since the early 1980s. Inasmuch as this can be interpreted as "revealed preferences" rather than, for instance, an unobserved common determinant (imported raw material prices, etc.), we can interpret this as convergence in preferences.

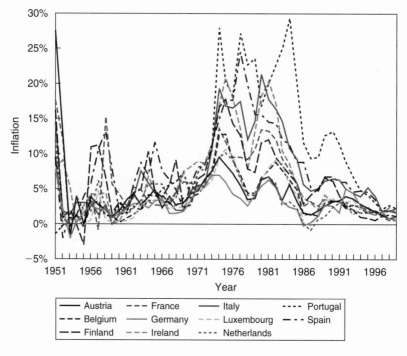

Figure 3.5
Inflation in EMU countries.

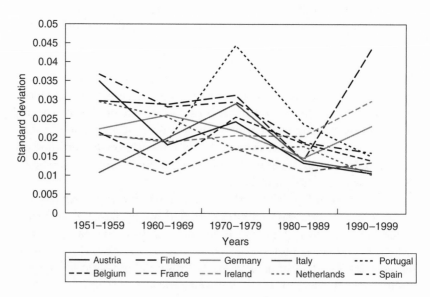

Figure 3.6
Standard deviation of real growth.

Can we say the same about the volatility of output? Following the logic of the standard monetary policy model (e.g., see section 3.2), we should expect an increase in the variance of real variables, as monetary policy puts greater weight on stable prices. Figure 3.6 reveals, however, that the evidence here is mixed. While the variance of real growth has been increasing in a number of euro zone countries at least since the late 1980s, it has been in decline in most ECB member countries. A possible explanation could be that, as already hinted at above, the observed reduction in average inflation during the last decade at least in part might have been due to exogenous influences rather than a systematic change in policy preferences alone.

Finally, we report the outcomes of a latent variables model to estimate conservativeness of the policy-makers in the euro zone countries. Most theoretical models (including our model in section 3.2) define the concept in terms of differences in priority with respect to inflation and output stabilization. A problem in dealing with the degree of conservativeness is that it is a variable that cannot be observed directly. Therefore Leertouwer et al. (2001) have used a latent variables approach. For the 1980s and the 1990s they have constructed an indicator for 14 OECD countries using inflation, the standard deviation of inflation, the standard deviation of output growth (corrected for terms of trade shocks), and the conservativeness as embodied in the central bank law (see table 3.7; the Cukierman index has been used) as "determinants" of conservativeness.[15] So this variable not only relies on legal information but also on actual behavior. The country scores as reported in table 3.9 have been calculated using the results of a factor analysis. This approach yields a variable that has, by definition, an average of zero and a standard deviation of one. In other words, the absolute values are of little interest. Still it is interesting to examine whether EMU countries have changed positions over time, and to analyze their relative positions. A number of conclusions can be drawn. First, some EMU countries (e.g., France) have become more conservative. Although some observers have argued that differences in preferences between France and Germany could pose a problem for the ECB, the results in table 3.9 do not lend support to this view. Second, some EMU countries (notably Italy, Spain, and Greece) have positions both in the 1980s and 1990s that are rather far away from the rest of the euro zone. In other words, these results suggest that within the ECB the main border line in terms of preferences is (still) between northern and southern European countries.

Table 3.9
Conservativeness of policy-makers in 14 OECD countries

Country	Score 1980s (ranking)	Score 1990s (ranking)
Austria	−1.139 (1)	−0.392 (7)
Germany	−1.049 (2)	−0.428 (5)
Belgium	−0.954 (3)	−0.504 (3)
Netherlands	−0.883 (4)	−0.378 (8)
France	−0.522 (5)	−0.607 (1)
Sweden	−0.505 (6)	−0.016 (10)
Denmark	−0.484 (7)	−0.513 (2)
Finland	−0.248 (8)	−0.504 (4)
Norway	−0.225 (9)	−0.373 (9)
United Kingdom	0.711 (10)	0.156 (11)
Ireland	1.135 (11)	−0.427 (6)
Italy	1.210 (12)	0.332 (12)
Spain	1.327 (13)	0.370 (13)
Greece	1.626 (14)	3.283 (14)

Source: Leertouwer et al. (2001).

3.6 Policy Conclusions

In comparison to the Bundesbank after the 1950s and the modern-day Fed, the ECB is very decentralized. Decentralized implementation of monetary policy may be useful, given the knowledge national central banks have of their own national financial markets and local institutional circumstances. However, an important question is whether the relatively large influence of national central banks in the decision-making process is warranted. This institutional setup may become worrisome if the economies of the euro zone countries diverge and/or if there are large differences in terms of preferences across policy-makers.

Our results suggest that business cycles in the euro zone countries have synchronized over time due to economic integration. The same seems to be true, with some qualifications, for the preferences of policy makers. However, there still exist substantial differences among the economies of the euro zone countries, and the experience of Germany and other monetary unions suggests that some differences are likely to remain. Moreover the case of the early German Bundesbank suggests that differences in national economic development might indeed lead to differences in voting behavior in the Governing Council. This suggests that current practices in the ECB to reach "policy decisions by consensus" may not last. These worries will only increase if in the near future the euro zone will be enlarged.

Various options come to mind to reduce the power of national central banks. As already pointed out, the Executive Board, for example, could be increased. Alternatively, the Board could have a say in appointing central bank presidents. Presently the ECB has no role in the selection of national central bank governors, which is a prerogative of the governments of the individual member states. In contrast, the Board of Governors of the Federal Reserve System has to give its approval to nominations of reserve bank presidents. The most far-reaching option is, of course, to introduce a system of weighted votes, where the weights reflect the economic importance of the countries. Perhaps the experience of the Fed may be helpful. One could introduce a rotating voting system like the FOMC has in the United States. All presidents of the central banks in the euro zone could participate in the policy discussions, but only a limited and rotating number of them has the right to cast a vote.

Notes

1. This contrasts with the Federal Reserve System where some specialization by the regional banks has been achieved. All open market operations, for instance, are carried out by the New York Fed, which is also responsible for the management of reserves and the implementation of foreign exchange interventions.

2. Although formally each national central bank president has one vote, during the discussions the position of the president of the Bundesbank, say, may be different from the president of the central bank of Luxembourg, say. Also personal characteristics and reputation of the various presidents may play a role in the decision-making process. These considerations imply that the political power of some presidents of national banks may be greater than those of others even though they have the same position in terms of formal voting rules.

3. The political weight carried by individual central bank representatives relative to the sum of national representatives is higher (1/12 or about 8 percent). The difference is due to the 6 members of the Executive Board. Consequently the political weight of a given country representative is decreasing in the number of members in the Executive Board that hold voting rights in the Governing Council.

4. It is a very simple model. Still, it is a nice way to illustrate some well-known points made in the literature about the risks of decentralization of the ECB. A related model that focuses on differences in the monetary transmission mechanism is Gros and Hefeker (2000).

5. Based on equations (3.2) and (3.4), following the same steps as described for the euro zone's monetary policy, we find that country R's first-best policy response would be $\pi_R = \alpha b_R \varepsilon_R / (1 + \alpha^2 b_R)$. In other words, the country would react to its domestic output shock alone. For $b_R = b_E$ this is just what we find in the limit for $\gamma \to 1$ in (3.8).

6. One could conjecture that if this is the case, why did countries join in the first place? It should be recalled, however, that other political considerations played a major role in many countries when they decided about EMU.

7. All economic data employed in this section has been provided by the statistical office of Baden-Württemberg and is available from the authors on request. Until 1957 the Bundesbank was named Bank deutscher Länder.

8. We also looked at Council minutes over the period 1962 to 1969 but found their information content too poor to extend the database.

9. It is difficult to interpret differences in the reaction of regions to real and nominal deviations from average as the model only refers to absolute region-to-average differences. We will return to this question below, however, where we investigate the direction of the dissent voting.

10. Presidents of regional central banks were nominated by the government of the Land concerned, while members of the Executive Board of the Bundesbank were nominated by the federal government.

11. This empirical finding is in line, for instance, with the theoretical predictions of new-Keynesian models such as laid out in Svensson (1999) or the Coricelli, Cukierman, and Dalmazzo (2003) model with endogenous trade union behavior.

12. The countries are Austria, Belgium, Canada, Denmark, Finland, France, Germany, Greece, Ireland, Italy, Japan, Netherlands, Norway, Spain, Sweden, Switzerland, the United Kingdom, and the United States.

13. With 18 countries and 4 periods there are $4 \cdot (18 \cdot 17)/2 = 612$ observations.

14. One additional approach not dealt with in the present chapter is the idea that European societies differ with regard to inflation culture and that this is reflected in their institutional setup. See, for example, Hayo (1998).

15. For the inflation, its standard deviation and the adjusted standard deviation of output growth both the average of the decade under consideration as well as the average of the previous decade were used.

References

Artis, M. J., and W. Zhang. 1997. International business cycles and the ERM: Is there a European business cycle? *International Journal of Finance and Economics* 2: 1–16.

Artis, M. J., and W. Zhang. 1999. Further evidence on the international business cycle and the ERM: Is there a European business cycle? *Oxford Economic Papers* 51: 120–32.

Berger, H. 1997. *Konjunkturpolitik im Wirtschaftswunder.* Tübingen: Mohr Siebeck.

Berger, H., and U. Woitek. 1999. Does conservatism matter? A time series approach to central banking. CESifo Working Paper 190.

Berger, H., J. De Haan, and S. C. W. Eijffinger. 2001. Central bank independence: An update of theory and empirical evidence. *Journal of Economic Surveys* 15: 3–40.

Cukierman, A. 1992. *Central Bank Strategy, Credibility, and Independence.* Cambridge: MIT Press.

De Grauwe, P. 2000a. *The Economics of Monetary Integration*. Oxford: Oxford University Press.

De Grauwe, P. 2000b. Monetary policies in the presence of asymmetries. CEPR Discussion Paper 2393.

Grilli, V., D. Masciandaro, and G. Tabellini. 1991. Political and monetary institutions and public financial policies in the industrial countries. *Economic Policy* (13): 341–92.

Gros, D., and C. Hefeker. 2000. One size must fit all: National divergences in a monetary union. CESifo Working Paper 326.

Haan, J. de, and W. Kooi. 1997. What really matters? Conservativeness or independence? *Banca Nazionale del Lavoro Quarterly Review* 200: 23–38.

Eijffinger, S. C. W., and J. de Haan. 2000. *European Monetary and Fiscal Policy*. Oxford: Oxford University Press.

Emerson, M., D. Gros, A. Italianer, J. Pisani-Ferry, and H. Reichenbach. 1992. *One Market, One Money*. Oxford: Oxford University Press.

Fatás, A. 1997. EMU: Countries or regions? Lessons from the EMS experience. *European Economic Review* 41: 743–51.

Fase, M. M. G., and W. Van't Hoor. 2000. Het Federal Reserve System Nader Bezien. Mimeo: De Nederlandsche Bank.

Frankel, J. A., and A. K. Rose. 1998. The endogeneity of the optimum currency area criteria. *Economic Journal* 108: 1009–25.

Hayo, B. 1998. Inflation culture, central bank independence and price stability. *European Journal of Political Economy* 14: 241–63.

Inklaar, R., and J. de Haan. 2001. Is there really a European business cycle? A Comment. *Oxford Economic Papers* 53: 215–20.

Kilponen, J. 1999. Central bank independence and wage bargaining structure—Empirical evidence. Bank of Finland Discussion Paper 9/99.

Krugman, P. 1991. *Geography and Trade*. Cambridge: MIT Press.

Leertouwer, E., J. de Haan, and H. Berger. 2001. How conservative are policymakers in the euro area? Mimeo: University of Groningen.

Sinn, H. W. 2001. Chancellor Schröder's "Steady Hand" must act now. *Ifo Viewpoint*, no. 29 (November 8, 2001).

Svensson, L. 1999. Inflation targeting as a monetary policy rule. *Journal of Monetary Economics* 43(3): 607–54.

Vaubel, R. 1997. The bureaucratic and partisan behaviour of independent central banks: German and international evidence. *European Journal of Political Economy* 13(2): 201–24.

Vaubel, R. 1999. The future of the euro: A public choice perspective. Mimeo: University of Mannheim.

Comment on Chapter 3

Mika Widgrén

Overall, I find De Haan, Berger, and Inklaar's discussion very interesting and important. In short, they argue that differences in national monetary preferences may cause problems under the current decision-making rules in the European Central Bank and lead to suboptimal monetary policy decisions. If monetary integration leads to convergence and hence increased business cycle synchronization in the euro area, the problems are likely to be less severe. However, whether convergence will take place is a priori unclear.

Using the federal German Bundesbank as an example the authors argue that differences in the economic situation in the various states have affected the voting behavior in the Governing Council despite the fact that business cycles in the German states have become quite similar over time. I think that this point touches the role of the institution design, which is unfortunately otherwise entirely left out of the chapter.

For the euro zone countries the chapter provides some evidence of increased business cycle synchronization and convergence of preferences. Still, important differences remain. As all national central banks have one vote within the Governing Council of the ECB, there is a risk that national considerations may prevail over euro-wide considerations. I find this argument convincing, but it seems that the chapter does not analyze the impact of the decentralized voting system far enough.

I think that as this point makes clear, a more careful general analysis of different voting rule designs in the Governing Council would have been a good additional element in the chapter to answer the question properly. Moreover the eastern enlargement of the EU, and subsequent enlargement of the EMU, is likely to increase the heterogeneity of monetary preferences in Euroland even further, which makes the topic more urgent.

One useful way to assess decision making in the Governing Council is to use a simple spatial voting model. In these models it is possible to assume differentiated (national) monetary preferences or to assess decision-making prospects in a broader more abstract sense. Then assuming that monetary preferences will differ from one decision maker to another in a single vote but that the distributions of ideal monetary decisions are the same, the setup can be used to consider how well the decision-making institution is likely to perform. Note that analyzing expected performance in this setup gives weight only to purely institutional factors in explaining different designs. There are no long-run asymmetries between national preferences.

In the current Governing Council (GC) of the ECB the Executive Board (EB) has six members, and in addition there are twelve national central bank governors (NCB). Decisions are made using a simple majority and in the case of a tie the vote of EB president is pivotal. To make the picture even simpler let us assume, as in Baldwin et al. (2001a, b), that EB members are interested in Euroland average and act in unison but that each NCB governor adopts a purely national perspective. Let us normalize the current state of affairs, namely the reference policy, to zero. Suppose that CG must decide on interest rate changes ranging from 25 to 50 basis points up or down. Let each governor in NCB have an ideal policy change on the interval from -0.5 percentage points to $+0.5$ percentage points after a random shock (for the details, see Baldwin et al. 2001b). The euro-zone average is now the weighted average of national ideal policy positions.

In the setup above, it turn out that the status quo bias, namely GC's disability to make any change from the status quo toward the weighted average, is approximately 4 percent in the current ECB, but it increases to 17 percent if we assume that all 27 future member states of the EU belong to the EMU. Note that these numbers assume symmetry among the countries. In sum, in addition to a potential problems that due to a decentralized decision making, the ECB is facing a numbers problem, like the Commission, in the future. Assuming asymmetries in the setup makes things still much more complicated in terms of reaching optimal policy outcomes and avoiding the status quo bias.

References

Baldwin, R., E. Berglöf, F. Giavazzi, and M. Widgrén. 2001a. Nice try: Should the treaty of Nice be ratified? *Monitoring European Integration* 11, Centre for Economic Policy Research, London.

Baldwin, R., E. Berglöf, F. Giavazzi, and M. Widgrén. 2001b. Preparing the ECB for enlargement. CEPR Policy Paper 6.

II   Fiscal and Financial
                          Aspects of European
                          Monetary Integration

4   Fiscal Aspects of Central Bank Independence

Christopher A. Sims

4.1 Introduction

There are two ideal models of a central bank, of which actual central banks are usually a mixture. In type F, which is close to describing the US Federal Reserve system, the central bank's balance sheet is always perfectly hedged, with short-term interest-bearing nominal bond assets and high-powered money liabilities that leave almost no risk of balance sheet problems. There is a single government budget constraint, reflecting the certainty that mature government bonds can always be redeemed for high-powered money and the fact that there is no doubt that potential central bank balance sheet problems are nothing more than a type of fiscal liability for the treasury.

In type E, which seems to be the model underlying the constitution of the ECB and which (in an extreme version) is close to matching currency-board arrangements like that in Hong Kong, the central bank holds assets whose return distributions do not match those of its liabilities but are intended to act as reserves, guaranteeing a lower bound on the value of its high-powered money liabilities in terms of some other store of value. In this model the central bank budget constraint is distinct from that of the treasury (or in the case of the ECB, treasuries). Mature nominal government debt might not, in some circumstances, be convertible at par into high-powered money, and conversely, it is not obvious that a treasury would automatically see central bank balance sheet problems as its own liability.

In either model, central bank policy actions aimed at controlling the price level have budgetary implications. There is a flow of interest earnings on assets held by the central bank that generally exceeds any interest it pays out on liabilities, most of which is usually turned over to the treasury. There may also be other cash flows between the central bank and the treasury as the bank buys and sells assets in the market. The essence of central bank independence is that these cash flows are regarded simply as by-products of a central bank monetary policy aimed at meeting its assigned policy objectives. There is no presumption that the treasury or the legislature requires a commitment from the central bank to provide specified or minimum cash flows.

In most advanced economies it is now the norm that the treasury is not allowed to require the central bank to purchase given amounts of treasury debt. Equally important, it is conventional nearly everywhere to treat the central bank's interest earnings as a residual item in the budget, with no discussion of targets for such revenue. In unusual but nonetheless important circumstances, however, central bank seignorage revenue, interpreted broadly as changes in its net worth, can become negative. The convention that other branches of government are not concerned with the level of the central bank's interest earnings does not usually extend to such cases of negative seignorage, and this fact constitutes a limitation on the level of independence available to the central bank.

In model F, this potential limitation is kept a very remote possibility by the structure of the bank balance sheet. Of course, surprise changes in asset prices can occur, but with assets that are short-term, interest-bearing, and denominated in the same units as nearly all of its liabilities, there is very little room for disparate movements in the values of the central bank's assets and liabilities.

In model E, the bank must balance a risk of negative shocks to its balance sheet against the principle that it should be capable of allowing and weathering a government default. It therefore acquires assets whose risks are not as perfectly correlated with those of its currency liabilities as with model E. Foreign exchange reserves, for example, are always subject to sudden revaluation, as are any securities issued by private entities. A model E central bank can minimize the risk of balance sheet problems by diversifying its portfolio of assets, by investing only in securities issued by the most sound and stable entities, and by building up net worth through incomplete rebate of interest earnings to the treasury. Each of these approaches, however, implies some important limits on the bank's freedom of action.

Another route by which model E independence might be undermined is the treatment of seignorage revenue. If bank net worth is not to grow exponentially, there must be a rule requiring that earnings in excess of expenses be turned over to a treasury (or some other entity). This is true of model F central banks as well, but for a model E bank the oversight may be less strong because of its weaker links to the treasury. Also, for a model E bank, the problems that would be created by negative net worth provide an apparent rationale for indefinite accumulation of positive net worth. But when this occurs, as in the Hong Kong case, the large positive net worth is likely itself to become a threat to bank independence. Political pressure to use the accumulated wealth for some worthwhile public purpose may be strong. If the seignorage is regularly turned over to the treasury, and if the revenue grows very large, the treasury is likely to come to depend on it and to apply pressure to avoid its shrinking. In defense, the central bank is likely to be tempted to expand its mission, for example by undertaking to be a backup source of liquidity for a growing list of types of financial institutions. But such "mission creep" exposes the bank to new risks and therefore again to limitations on its ability to control the price level.[1]

Both ideal models can provide a stable price level, and the differences between them may not appear important in normal times. But in any general equilibrium model, uniqueness and stability of the price level depends on beliefs of the public about how the system would react in the face of extreme circumstances like very high inflation, severe financial instability, or deflations in which the zero lower bound on nominal interest rates is approached. The kind of behavior required of the central bank and the treasury in such circumstances is different under the two models. Because of these differences, the ability of severe disturbances to force policy-makers to allow a deviation from price stability also differs across the two models.

4.2 Informal Discussion of Conditions for Existence and Uniqueness

We will consider an economy in which barter equilibrium, with real balances zero, is a nontrivial possibility. This could be because use of a foreign currency for transactions is possible, or because electronic payments systems could expand greatly if the cost of holding money was held high enough, or simply because people are ingenious (as recently in certain sectors of the Russian economy).

Suppose that monetary policy simply fixes $M = \bar{M}$, where M is the quantity of non-interest-bearing currency. If there are no disturbances to the economy, this policy is likely to be consistent with a unique, constant price level, under either model of the central bank. However, it is also generally consistent with the pure barter equilibrium in which money is valueless. Monetary theory has made it clear by now that these are usually not the only two equilibria. Usually there is a continuum of equilibria, one for every initial value of the price level above the level $\bar{p}$ that is consistent with constant p. In each of these equilibria the price level explodes upward, velocity explodes upward, and real balances shrink toward zero, so the economy approaches barter.

These explosive equilibria can be eliminated if the fixed-M policy is supplemented with a commitment to support the value of money at some ceiling level of prices $P = P^*$. The policy would be that the central bank or the treasury would stand ready to sell arbitrary amounts of real goods in return for money at the price P^*. The model E central bank can make such a commitment if it owns a stock F of a "real" asset, and if it has chosen P^* such that $\bar{M}/P^* < F$. Note that it requires no assist from the treasury in making such a commitment and that there is no requirement that $\bar{M}/\bar{P} < F$. The bank can be at negative net worth all the time. Because speculators know that the bank's commitment to redeem money will not come into play until the price level has risen to P^*, the speculators can see that the explosive paths are not sustainable, which will force any initial $P > \bar{P}$ immediately back down to $\bar{P}$.

An economy with a model F central bank can also rule out these explosive demonetization equilibria, but to do so requires treasury intervention. Because on the inflation path the assets of the bank are shrinking as fast as its liabilities, the ratio of its net worth to the value of M will not grow as inflation proceeds. A credible commitment to redeem money at P^* requires a commitment to use the power to tax.

As recently pointed out by Benhabib, Schmitt-Grohe, and Uribe (1998), indeterminacy problems can also arise as uncontrollable deflations, with interest rates stuck at zero. If we pay no attention to fiscal policy, this outcome seems a remote possibility with an $M = \bar{M}$ policy, as the real value of currency outstanding increases without bound as price drops, and the resulting wealth effect should make the downward spiral unsustainable. Benhabib, Schmitt-Grohe, and Uribe get their result by assuming that the fiscal authority treats the rising real value of central bank liabilities as treasury liabilities that must be backed with taxation, thereby offsetting the real balance effect on private wealth. As the recent example of Japan shows, this type of fiscal reaction to deflation is not as implausible as it sounds at first. Of course, in Japan there have been large fiscal deficits, but these are accompanied by rhetoric about what a large burden of future taxation or reduced expenditure these deficits imply. Furthermore a central bank concerned about its deteriorating balance sheet can take quasi-fiscal actions that contribute to further deflation. An example is the sharp increase in reserve requirements imposed by the US Federal Reserve before the 1937 recession. A bank with such concerns could also hoard interest earnings and refrain from bold, risky open market purchases to sustain fiscal institutions or end the deflation.

Since this kind of indeterminacy is primarily a problem of bad fiscal policy, models E and F do not directly imply different outcomes here. However, to the extent that the central bank has the power to make risky open market purchases to end the deflation, it requires an understanding that it will if necessary have fiscal backing. This is a natural possibility (if not at all inevitable) for a model F bank. For a model E bank it apparently violates the essence of its "independence." Such a bank might therefore be more likely to see no feasible action available to it in a liquidity trap.

Another simple policy is a pure price peg. Of course, such a policy presents implementation problems in practice, but assume for now that it is possible.[2] A bank with positive net worth can implement a price peg. The peg will not be subject to speculative attack because of the net worth cushion. But as soon as the bank's net worth becomes negative at the pegged price, it becomes unsustainable and multiple equilibria, corresponding to the possibility of random speculative attack that demonetizes the economy, arise. Obviously a type F bank, because it is much more reliably cushioned against negative net worth, is more likely to be able to sustain a price peg.

Finally, there is the possibility of a pure nominal interest rate peg. It is one of the main novel results of the fiscal theory of the price level that such equilibria are sustainable, with stable prices, if fiscal policy is appropriate. For a type F bank the interest rate peg becomes in effect a commitment to monetize a fixed fraction of variation in the level of nominal debt, and prices become proportional to the quantity of nominal debt. This requires that the fiscal authorities generate a "nominal anchor," by not basing their rule for real taxation on a measure of real debt outstanding. This type of equilibrium obviously requires tight coordination between the central bank and fiscal authorities, and it is therefore inconsistent with the type E model. It is likely to imply a less smooth path for the price level than a price-targeting policy or a fixed-M policy, but it has the appeal that it narrows the amplitude of swings in the level of taxation compared to the other equilibria, which is appealing on efficiency grounds if taxes are distorting.[3]

We can summarize the implications of these discussions as follows: A type F central bank depends on fiscal cooperation and backup under certain conditions if it is to guarantee a stable price level. If it can rely on such backup, it will need to invoke it only very rarely, so its effective degree of independence may be great. A type E bank can do without fiscal backup under certain conditions in which a type F bank would need it. But in a much broader set of conditions, a type E bank will find that the need to maintain or attain positive net worth is a constraint on its ability to tightly control the price level.

There is no unique answer as to which model will perform better. In an economy where the political system and fiscal expertise are low, the coordination and restraint required of the treasury by a type F arrangement may not be available and the type E model may therefore be more attractive. Certainly currency boards, which are a type E arrangement, are more common in less developed countries. One would think that in an economy as advance as that of euroland, type F would be the natural model. But since the ECB has a multitude of treasuries to deal with, it is quite understandable that in the initial stages it is framed as a type E bank.

4.3   Models F and E in General Equilibrium

Our aim here is not to prove results in great generality, but to provide a simple model within which the intertemporal equilibrium mechanisms are transparent. We can reach some conclusions without being explicit about which type of central bank is present in the model.[4] We suppose an economy with a representative agent maximizing

$$\int_0^\infty e^{-\beta t} \log C_t \, dt \tag{4.1}$$

with respect to the time paths of C, F_P, B and M, subject to the constraint

$$C(1 + \psi(v)) + \dot{F}_P + \frac{\dot{M} + \dot{B}}{P} = Y + \rho F_P + \frac{\dot{B}}{P} + \tau. \tag{4.2}$$

Here C is consumption, $v = PC/M$ is velocity of money, F_P is private holdings of the real asset, B is nominal government debt, M is money (non-interest-bearing currency), Y is an exogenous endowment stream, and τ is transfer payments from the government. The real and nominal interest rates are, respectively, ρ and τ.

The first-order conditions for the private agent are

$$\partial B: \quad \frac{\lambda}{P}\left(-\frac{\dot{\lambda}}{\lambda} + \beta + \frac{\dot{P}}{P}\right) = \frac{r\lambda}{P}, \tag{4.3}$$

$$\partial F: \quad -\dot{\lambda} + \beta\lambda = \rho\lambda, \tag{4.4}$$

$$\partial M: \quad \frac{\lambda}{P}\left(-\frac{\dot{\lambda}}{\lambda} + \beta + \frac{\dot{P}}{P}\right) = \frac{\lambda}{P}\psi'v^2, \tag{4.5}$$

$$\partial C: \quad C^{-1} = \lambda(1 + \psi + \psi'v). \tag{4.6}$$

These equations can be reduced to

$$r = \rho + \frac{\dot{P}}{P}, \tag{4.7}$$

$$r = \psi'v^2, \tag{4.8}$$

$$\rho - \beta = \frac{\dot{C}}{C} + \frac{(2\psi' + \psi''v^2)\dot{v}}{1 + \psi + \psi'v}. \tag{4.9}$$

Note that in all these equations we are supposing that the economy evolves without uncertainty after $t = 0$ but that some variables may change discontinuously at $t = 0$. Thus all time derivatives (dotted variables) are to be interpreted as right-derivatives.

Now suppose that the monetary authority adopts an "active" monetary policy in the terminology of Leeper (1991), for example, that it targets the price level, using an interest rate instrument. Such a policy could take the form of setting the nominal interest rate according to

$$r = \theta_0 + \theta_1 p, \tag{4.10}$$

where p is the log of the price level. Combining (4.10) with (4.7) gives us

$$\dot{p} = \theta_0 + \theta_1 p - \rho. \tag{4.11}$$

We will suppose that ρ is set exogenously, and is constant except possibly for a discontinuous change at $t = 0$. Equation (4.11) is easily seen to be an unstable equation with a unique nonexplosive solution:

$$p \equiv \bar{p} = \frac{\rho - \theta_0}{\theta_1}. \tag{4.12}$$

If the initial value of p exceeds $\bar{p}$, p explodes exponentially upward, while if the initial value is below $\bar{p}$, it explodes downward.

Notice that if the explosive paths are not equilibria, the price level is constant in equilibrium regardless of the size of θ_1, so long as it is positive. That is, the response of interest rates to price level changes can be as small as we like without altering the conclusion that the price level is constant. However, if we consider the effects of an exogenous shift in ρ at $t = 0$, the conclusion is different. It is natural to suppose that the monetary authority cannot accurately track the real rate, so it will not be able to offset changes in it by changing θ_0. In this case equation (4.12) can be read as describing how p reacts to exogenous shifts in ρ, and we can see that the amount of price change produced by a shift in ρ is smaller, the larger is θ_1. That is, by moving the nominal rate aggressively in response to changes in the price level, the monetary authority can keep the price level more stable in the presence of exogenous variation in the real rate.

Now we must consider whether it is indeed possible to exclude the explosive paths for the price level as possible equilibria. To illustrate how the model works, we consider the case of

$$\psi(v) = \frac{\psi_0 v}{1 + v}. \tag{4.13}$$

This specification implies that as $v \to \infty$, transactions costs converge to a finite limit, so that a barter equilibrium, with zero real balances, is technologically viable. In this setting (4.8) becomes

$$r = \frac{\psi_0 v^2}{(1 + v)^2}, \tag{4.14}$$

and it is then easily seen that we can satisfy this equation and (4.11) in the stable, constant-price equilibrium only if $\psi_0 > \rho$.

Assuming that this condition is met, it is still possible for the economy to start on a path for which initial $p > \bar{p}$, which would require that r rise steadily. But in this model, with this interest rate policy, there is an upper bound on p because, as $v \to \infty$, $r \to \psi_0$. That is, there is a level r^* of the nominal rate corresponding, via the policy equation, to a level p^* of the log price level, at which the public altogether gives up the use of currency for transactions purposes. When M has reached zero, the monetary authority can no longer continue with conventional interest rate policy, so to characterize equilibrium, we need to describe monetary policy behavior once $M = 0$.

One kind of modified policy that works here is a commitment to supply reserves F in return for currency at some price ratio $\bar{\bar{p}} < p^*$ at any time. If this commitment is credible, it undermines the speculative dynamics that support the explosive price paths. These paths can exist only because expectations of continued inflation, make high nominal interest rates and low real balances attractive to private agents. If there is an upper bound $\bar{\bar{p}}$ to p, then as the bound is reached, expectations of reduced inflation will tend to increase demand for money, thereby pushing down the price level. Foreseeing this, markets will push the price level down even earlier, and so on, leaving us with no upwardly explosive paths as equilibria.

But is it credible that the monetary authority can provide F in return for M at the price level p^*? A model F central bank can do so if it is tightly linked to a treasury with untapped powers to tax. Such a treasury can issue interest-bearing debt that implies a credible commitment to future taxation, and the real value of this debt will be stable. It can supply such debt to the central bank as fresh injections of capital in the event that the bank were to run out of its own holdings of assets. For a model E central bank, the answer to the question depends on its balance sheet position. It is not required that the bank have positive net worth at the price level $p = \bar{p}$. By the time the price level has reached $\bar{\bar{p}} > \bar{p}$, the real value of the bank's original liabilities will have been reduced, while the assets it holds in the form of F will have retained their value. Along a path on which r and p explode upward, the bank will have to be selling reserves to absorb M in order to keep r rising according to its policy. Its commitment to a price ceiling at $\bar{\bar{p}}$ is credible if its reserves are sufficient to absorb the whole money stock along such a path. If $\bar{\bar{p}}$ is enough larger than $\bar{p}$, the commitment can be credible even with substantially negative net worth for the bank at $p = \bar{p}$. And with a credible commitment, the explosive paths are eliminated as potential equilibria, so the reserves are never called upon.

Of course, if the reserves are not sufficient, then this interest rate policy is subject to the same kind of speculative attack, multiple equilibrium scenario as the pure price peg. We can find from equations we have already derived that

$$\bar{\bar{p}} - \bar{p} < \frac{\psi_0 - \rho}{\theta_1}. \tag{4.15}$$

That is, the percentage deviation above the stable price level at which demonetization is complete is a decreasing function of θ_1. Thus in place of the extreme result we obtained informally in discussing a price-pegging policy, we obtain a more continuous analogue: the more tightly the central bank attempts to control the price level with interest rates, the more sensitive it is to a blow to its net worth.

While we now have the main results from this model that interest us, we have computed only part of the equilibrium. It may not be obvious that there is a complete equilibrium for an arbitrary exogenously fixed ρ. However, we do know that if equilibrium exists under the price targeting policy, it will involve constant prices, and therefore from (4.7) $r = \rho$. Then from the liquidity preference relation (4.8) and the definition of ψ (4.13), we can find the constant equilibrium value of v, which we can call $\bar{v}$. Then turning to (4.9) we see that with v constant we will have $\dot{C}/C = \rho - \beta$ constant as well. Thus, if ρ increases from an initial value of β, we shift from an equilibrium with constant C to one with exponentially growing C. Since P and v are constant, M must grow in proportion to C.

Is such a growth path for C technically feasible? Under the assumption that real assets F can be borrowed or purchased from abroad and pay a fixed real rate ρ, the increase in ρ will cause an initial drop in C, followed by steady growth that can be financed by a growing holding of real assets.

4.4   Central Bank Independence as Historical Reality

4.4.1   Are ECB and the Fed Actual Examples of E and F?

This chapter has suggested that its type E and F categories correspond to the ECB and the US Federal Reserve. This may be controversial, but it has at least some superficial plausibility. The documents defining the ECB make it very clear that it is not to hold directly debt issued by the EMU treasuries. They discuss explicitly the possibility that countries that run irresponsible fiscal policies will find themselves paying premiums on their borrowing rates, which the ECB is committed not to eliminate. Such premia could arise only if markets contemplate the possibility that government debt might not be redeemable at par in some eventuality—that is, that governments could default. Conversely, the very fact that there is a host of fiscal authorities that would have to co-ordinate in order to provide backup were the ECB to develop balance sheet problems suggests that such backup is at least more uncertain than in the United States. And finally the balance sheet of the European

System of central banks shows (in the November 2000 issue of the *Monthly Bulletin* of the ECB, table 1) that 54 percent of the system's assets are non-euro-denominated, more than enough to back all outstanding currency with non-euro assets.

In contrast, the US Federal Reserve System manages the marketing of US federal government debt, making the notion of its failing to redeem mature debt at par seem bizarre, though not impossible. For a long time Treasury notes circulated alongside Federal Reserve notes as currency in the United States. Though this is no longer the case, I think that there is still no legal barrier to the Treasury's deciding, if necessary, to issue non-interest-bearing notes of modest denomination, which adds to the difficulty of imagining Treasury securities not being redeemable at par in nominal terms. The Federal Reserve System, according to its 1999 86th annual report, had only 4.9 percent of its assets in foreign-denominated form, which is only a very small fraction of its outstanding currency liabilities.

The Fed carries just 1.9 percent of its balance sheet in capital and reserves, while the ECB has 6.7 percent in this category.[5]

All these differences fit the pattern I have suggested for type F and E approaches to institutionalizing central bank independence, though of course there remains plenty of room for disagreement.

4.2.2   Mexico, Japan, and Grover Cleveland

It is now widely accepted that the Japanese central bank has in recent years been slow to move against persistent deflation in part because of fears about what some suggested bold interventions might do to its balance sheet. According to its November 2000 balance sheet, as reported on its Web site at *http://www.boj.or.jp/en/dlong_f.htm*, the Bank of Japan is close to the type F model. It has only 3.5 percent of its assets in foreign reserves, and less than 5 percent of its balance sheet in net worth. It has been suggested that the Bank make massive purchases of long-term debt, or of foreign currency. Either of these courses of action would leave its balance sheet subject to sudden revaluation. The former would almost automatically create difficulties if it succeeded in undoing deflationary expectations, thereby reducing bond prices. The latter would tend to improve the bank's balance sheet if it created the desired inflation and (thereby) devaluation, but because of the inherent unpredictability of exchange rates would nonetheless create balance sheet risk. Either would require moving away from the type F model of a risk-matched balance sheet with minimal risk of losing net worth.

The Bank of Mexico at the time of its last major crisis undertook long-term swap agreements with private banks, taking private loans off their hands in return for government securities. As these agreements have expired, the private banks fear that their viability will be impaired by the return of the now-questionable loans. A fiscal bailout has been proposed, but in part because the loans were in many cases to influential members of the formerly dominant political party, it has been extremely controversial. While I know of no obvious effect of this situation on Bank of Mexico policy, it is clear that it is a situation that could make the bank in future think twice about a similar intervention. Nearly any attempt to shore up confidence in a fiscal crisis by discounting privately issued securities will face a central bank with the risk of a situation like this, in which fiscal backing could prove necessary.

4.5   Conclusion

What are the implications of the point of view developed in this chapter for the structure and policy of the ECB? For the ECB itself, there is no implied critique of their existing framework. In fact, once we see the ECB as a type E bank, their reluctance to fully embrace inflation targeting and their apparent affection for considering the quantity of money as one "pillar" of policy are more understandable. As we have seen, aggressive inflation-targeting[6] carries serious risks for a type E bank, while stabilizing the quantity of money is less likely to generate balance sheet problems.

But for the European community as a whole, this analysis brings out some unresolved problems that deserve attention. To help the ECB evolve toward the more stable type F model, and thereby to help it compete as a world reserve currency, the EMU will need to develop fiscal institutions capable of prompt and strong actions at a Europe-wide level. This is a tall order, so it may not be filled any time soon, unless a financial crisis forces some rapid political innovation. It might be worthwhile for Europe to consider creating a fiscal emergency system to be invoked only in time of financial crisis. This, since it would be thought of as a backstop to be rarely if ever used, might be easier to negotiate than a broader fiscal integration. Lars Svensson has informed me that at least at one point in history, part of the legislation defining the Swedish central bank was that the bank could require the treasury to issue interest-bearing debt to use in replenishing a gap in net worth. In Europe, any facility like this would have to be negotiated in advance, to spread the fiscal burden across nations fairly. But it seems a valuable arrangement to have made, and perhaps not so difficult to achieve.

The other side of this issue is that while it is still in type E mode, the ECB will be constantly tempted to let its balance sheet and net worth grow, to make the prospect of balance sheet difficulties more remote. If the temptation is not resisted, this could create serious problems in the long run, both for the bank and for the European political system. A very large accumulation of wealth in the center of a system with weak political institutions is an invitation to trouble.

Notes

1. See Kwan and Lui (1999) for a discussion of the evolution of the Hong Kong exchange fund and the ambiguity of its mission.

2. We will see below that price level targeting via an interest rate instrument gives qualitatively similar results.

3. See Sims (1999a) and references therein.

4. Model F is dealt with in detail in other papers. Closest to this one in ideas and motivation is Sims (1999b), but see also Sims (1997). This chapter's theory differs in that it considers model E and in that it allows the private sector to borrow and lend externally at a fixed real rate.

5. Plus another 17.5 percent in "revaluation accounts," whose meaning I'm not sure of. If they are accumulated capital gains, they belong with the capital and reserves for current purposes and would push the total to 24.2 percent.

6. We have actually seen this only for price level targeting, but at least some forms of inflation targeting would have similar implications.

References

Benhabib, J., S. Schmitt-Grohe, and M. Uribe. 2001. Monetary policy and multiple equilibria. *American Economic Review* 91: 167–86.

Kwan, Y. K., and F. T. Lui. 1999. Hong Kong's currency board and changing monetary regimes. In T. Ito, and A. Krueger, eds., *Changes in Exchange Rates in Rapidly Developing Countries*, Chicago: University of Chicago Press.

Leeper, E. M. 1991. Equilibria under active and passive monetary and fiscal policies. *Journal of Monetary Economics* 27: 129–47.

Sims, C. A. 1997. Fiscal foundations of price stability in open economies. Discussion Paper. Department of Economics, Princeton University. *http://www.princeton.edu/sims/*.

Sims, C. A. 1999. The precarious fiscal foundations of EMU, *De Economist* 147(4): 415–36. *http://www.princeton.edu/sims/*.

Sims, C. A. 2001. Fiscal consequences for Mexico of adopting the dollar. *Journal of Money, Credit, and Banking*, 33 (2, pt. 2): 597–616. *http://www.princeton.edu/sims/*.

Comment on Chapter 4

Svend E. Hougaard Jensen

As I understand it, the issue Sims raises is whether the independence of a central bank could be compromised by so-called adverse balance sheet effects. This risk arises when a central bank faces a divided set of fiscal authorities who do not "own" the central bank and whose commitment to honor their own budget constraint might be weaker than elsewhere. The reason is that they could bet on some help in being bailed out, because that would be preferable to the partners, rather than having a liquidity crisis that might trigger further balance sheet problems at the common central bank and thereby worsen economic conditions and hence foul up their own budget constraints. In such a situation the economy could enter a high inflation spiral. This point is an interesting one, which to my knowledge has never really been addressed in the literature. Also, as central bank independence has become much prized and is generally regarded as a crucial for macroeconomic stability, the chapter may have some important policy implications.

The analysis would certainly be relevant in the context of the European Central Bank (ECB). Indeed, it could be argued that the problem pointed out by Sims offers an interesting, and novel, interpretation of the Stability and Growth Pact (SGP) in the European Monetary Union (EMU), in the sense that the SGP may be seen an attempt to prevent the ECB from running into these balance sheet problems. From that perspective, the recent exoneration of Germany and Portugal is a real setback, which might seriously compromise the SGPs credibility as a sanction mechanism. The story could also be of relevance to the US Federal Reserve System (the Fed), although the "instability scenario" would apply much less to that kind of central bank. However, it must apply to some extent to the Fed, or would do if the so-called balanced budget amendments were not in place.

Hence Sims' argument can be said to provide a possible new interpretation for the real motivation for implementing the balanced budget
amendments, which can therefore be seen as the attempt made by the
United States to prevent any of the adverse balance sheet effects. The
very obvious refusal to bail out New York City when it went bankrupt
in the 1970s and again in the 1980s can be seen in the same vein.

One could then ask whether all of this really matters much in practice? Well, I think it is difficult to find evidence to support the empirical
relevance of this analysis. First, the United States has not faced a case
where the assets held by the Fed have been seriously damaged by one
big state such as California failing to honor its budget constraints after
a major crisis in, say, the utilities. Nor has the ECB faced a problem with
a budget failure in, say, Italy (a similar sized component of the overall
economy). The difference is that in the US case, the federal government
could (and presumably would) arrange a quasi-bailout using federal
taxation (67 percent of all taxation), whereas Europe cannot: first,
because federal taxation in the EU only amounts to 3 percent of the total
and, second, because there is no forum in which a common fiscal solution could be agreed.

Let me point out some possible implications. First, if adverse balance
sheet effects pose an important risk in practice, this might be an important motive for not only having but also sticking to the SGP in the EMU.
However, one would again welcome some evidence demonstrating
whether this is an important risk, because it is really very hard for the
outsider to judge the reality of it. For example, how many central banks
have gone bankrupt in history? Not a lot, I suppose. Second, if the first
is important, this is another very important reason why the EU will find
out that it has to move to a common fiscal policy, whether with harmonized rates or not. Third, of course the actual comparitor at the opposite
end of the spectrum is a unified state (France or the United Kingdom)
with less federalism. But I suppose the United States is all right because
it has enough centralization to make the point.

Finally, the reason why I remain sceptical about the practical relevance of the problem is that it only really arises in periods of extreme
boom, if I understood correctly. In a slump, the real value of the bank's
assets is increasing, or at least falling no faster than its obligations, unless you think there will never be an upturn within the maturity of
those assets. But even in this circumstance the bank can print money.
Nobody cares because inflation is negative anyway; Japan is a case in

point. But in an extended boom, the central bank does have a problem if its assets are deemed worthless because nobody thinks the authorities (i.e., governments in the EU) will tax enough in the future to redeem those assets when they are due, so none will buy them when the ECB tries to sell them to reduce the money supply. But would not even a weak SGP force that? And, anyway, how often would one suppose that a tough ECB constitutionally committed to create price stability would allow such an extended boom to come about such that this became a significant problem? Not often, really. So I agree with Sims that the real danger is that the ECB would perhaps perceive this as an indirect threat to its independence. A Treasury in trouble would use this problem to blackmail the ECB into loosening its policies. And that as a result it would react by creaming off too much seigniorage revenue as a defense fund and getting too tight a set of policies as a result. Or that it would only hold assets of the most fiscally conservative governments, in which case it would presumably induce a risk premium on the interest rates of the others, weakening the common nature of the single monetary policy and placing the others at a disadvantage, or removing the problem if they got conservative too.

Notes

I gratefully acknowledge financial assistance from the Danish Ministry of Economics and Business Affairs and the Danish National Research Foundation. Opinions expressed are strictly my own, and should not be assumed to be those of my sponsors.

5

Seignorage Wealth in the Eurosystem: Eurowinners and Eurolosers Revisited

Hans-Werner Sinn
and Holger Feist

The rules laid down in Article 32 of the Protocol No. 18 on the Statute of the European System of Central Banks and of the European Central Bank of the Maastricht Treaty significantly redistribute European seignorage income and hence the implicit entitlement to the €352 billion stock of interest-bearing assets that the central banks contributed to the currency union as of January 1, 1999. By the ECB decision of December 6, 2001, the redistribution was started on January 1, 2003. In terms of wealth equivalents and anticipating the Greek participation, Germany loses €30 billion (or 59 billion deutschmarks) and France gains €31 billion (or 202 billion French francs). Portugal gains €3.9 billion (or 792 billion escudos) and Spain loses €11 billion (or 1,879 billion pesetas). In per capita terms, Luxembourg, Finland, and France are the main winners with gains of €1,309, €627, and €527, respectively, whereas a German loses €366 and a Spaniard €287. In this chapter we argue that this redistribution was not intended by the signing parties and recommend a revision of the Maastricht Treaty to correct the mistake.

5.1 Introduction

The European Monetary Union (EMU) socializes not only the goodwill and esteem that the national currencies have acquired but also the seignorage profit which the central banks earn by lending their money to the private sector at the market rate of interest. Throughout their histories central banks have accumulated interest-bearing assets step by step with the expansion of their respective monetary base which has followed the development of the economy. These assets, which total about €350 billion in the 11 euro countries, are stocks of "historic" seignorage wealth that generate an annual stream of returns and help finance government budgets. In January 1, 2002, the seignorage wealth of participating countries was brought into, and socialized by, the currency union.

The socialization of historic seignorage wealth did not occur in a legal sense, since only the future interest income generated by this wealth was pooled and redistributed. The national central banks remain the legal owners of the assets backing the monetary base. However, from an economic point of view, the eternal socialization of an asset's return is the same as the socialization of the asset itself. Thus, in economic terms, there was a once and for all socialization of current central bank assets.

In general, socialization involves an effective net redistribution among the participating countries because the interest income received by a country may differ from what this country contributes. A country's share in the interest contribution to the pool depends on its share in the joint monetary base. However, the share in the interest received from the pool is given by the average of this country's population and GDP shares. A country whose monetary base at the start of the currency union was large relative to its size as measured by these two indicators will lose, and a country whose monetary base was relatively small will gain. A losing country could be one whose currency is widely used outside its own borders or whose black market activities imply an unusually large usage of cash payments. This was noted in Remsperger (1996) and studied extensively in Sinn and Feist (1997) and Gros (1998). Not knowing precisely which countries would eventually participate in the currency union and what the stock of seignorage wealth would be at the start of this union, Sinn and Feist estimated gains and losses of up to €34 billion per country.

The redistribution of historic seignorage wealth was implied, though not openly spelled out, by Article 32 of the Protocol No. 18 (ex No. 3) on the Statute of the European System of Central Banks and of the European Central Bank (ECB) of the Maastricht Treaty. It seems fair to say that it was not understood and foreseen by the parties signing the treaty. It was only after the above-mentioned publications that politicians realized what they had signed, and the reaction was to postpone the beginning of the redistribution process by three years to clarify the matter. In 1998 the Governing Council of the ECB decided not to start the five-year transition period envisaged in Article 51 with the establishment of the currency union as of January 1, 1999. According to Article 32.3, transitional provisions were agreed on, as are discussed in more detail below, but they in effect only postponed the start of the redistribution process. The discussions about these rules received new momentum in the autumn of 2000.

5.2   The Scope of the Study

The Bundesbank (2000) was asked how much the introduction of the euro would cost the taxpayer. This simple, but far-reaching question could not be answered, because the future monetary development of the countries could not be forecasted with and without the currency union. Here we answer a more limited question that becomes clear as three categories of seignorage wealth are considered:[1]

1. Historic seignorage wealth built up before January 1, 1999.

2. The present value of increments in seignorage wealth that would have been built up by the single countries after January 1, 1999, had there not been a currency union.

3. The present value of additional increments in seignorage wealth, if any, that was generated after January 1, 1999, when the euro became more widely used outside Europe than the sum of the national currencies would have been without the currency union.

To answer the Bundesbank's question, a country's distributional gains and losses over all three of these categories would have had to be netted out. This was close to impossible since the required data were not available: partly because the analysis involved would be counterfactual, partly because knowledge was lacking about the euro's future. In this article we confine our attention to category 1 and try to show out how the distribution of historic seignorage wealth would be affected by the currency union.

There are two reasons for this limitation of scope. First, we want to produce cautious and unambiguous estimates of the redistributive wealth effects in order not to dramatize the issue. The figures under category 2 could be much larger in present value terms than those calculated under category 1, but under the assumption of identical growth rates of the national monetary bases they would just blow them up proportionately.[2]

Second, even if a country's gains under category 3 overcompensate any losses under category 1 and/or 2, it is not clear that they legitimate

such losses. It could well be argued that the extra increment in seignorage wealth, if any, which is due to the success of the euro should be
distributed equally among the participating Europeans. That some
Europeans gain more from the euro than others because they also gain
from the socialization of interest-bearing assets the others possessed
before the euro was introduced will be hard to understand for many
taxpayers.

Apart from that it is by no means clear that there have been gains of
type 3. Until the end of 2001, the euro suffered from a flight of money
holders outside the EU-11 countries from the deutschmark into the
dollar, which amounted to a huge destruction of European seignorage
wealth. The flight can probably be attributed to the three-year delay
between the announcement of the abolishment of the deutschmark and
introduction of the new currency. With the arrival of the new bank
notes and coins in January 2002, this flight stopped, and the amount
of currency in circulation is now increasing again, as recent ECB data
show.

The novelty of this article relative to the previous literature is three-
fold. First, it will offer redistributive figures that are calculated on the
basis of the official final balance sheets of the countries introducing
the euro rather than on estimates about these balance sheets. Second, it
can use the knowledge of who actually participates in the euro, a question that was not clear when the original calculations were made. Third,
it will calculate the incremental redistributive effects of the countries
that may join the EMU in the future.

5.3   Seignorage Wealth and Country Size

It is not easy to understand why central bank money is seignorage
wealth, because accounting practices blur the picture. The currency issued by a central bank is listed on the liability side of its balance sheet,
and the assets obtained in exchange for the currency are listed on the
asset side. From an accounting perspective, money creation does
not generate wealth with a central bank, because both sides of the
bank's balance sheet grow simultaneously without generating any differential equity capital. Indeed, this accounting custom may be the
reason why the signing parties did not really understand that they
were redistributing existing wealth when they founded the currency
union.

However, the point is that, in general, the central bank does not pay interest on the currency it issued while it collects interest on the assets obtained in exchange—the seignorage profit. The seignorage profit results from the return on the assets backing the outstanding stock of currency, and these assets are the seignorage wealth. From an economic perspective, seignorage wealth is a net wealth of the central banks because the stock of outstanding currency will never have to be serviced with interest payments or redemptions.[3]

As mentioned above, the eternal socialization of an asset's return is the same as the socialization of the asset itself. This fact enables us to base our calculations on the socialization of seignorage wealth rather than interest income. From a theoretical perspective there is little difference in focusing on interest income or seignorage wealth because the latter is the present value of the former. However, from a practical perspective the difference is large, since an interest-based calculation would involve an estimate of the time path of the average interest rate applicable to the assets backing the outstanding stock of currency.[4] The wealth approach avoids this difficulty. A country's seignorage wealth equals this country's stock of currency to the very last cent, and it is precisely equal to the present value of the interest income the backing assets generate, even though the time path of the average rate of interest for these assets may not be known.[5]

Under certain conditions the stock of a country's seignorage wealth is equal to its monetary base, namely the sum of coins, bank notes, and private accounts with the central banking system. However, in the present context some qualifications are necessary. Before the currency union it was a matter of debate whether the reserves that private banks are required to hold with the central bank should be counted as part of the central banks' seignorage wealth. Some countries imposed large reserve requirements, others imposed low or no requirements; some countries paid interest on the reserves held with the central bank, others did not.[6] This ambiguity has disappeared in the European currency system because the required minimum reserves with the central bank have been harmonized and the central banks now uniformly pay interest on them. The reserve requirement is 2 percent of a base that consists of time deposits with a maturity of no more than two years, of debt securities, and of money market papers. Banks are granted an interest rate which equals the average of the ECB's rates on the euro system's main refinancing operations; this rate is currently 2.0 percent. The minimum reserves therefore cannot be counted as net seignorage wealth, and they are subtracted in our calculations. Voluntary, non-interest-bearing reserves in excess of the minimum reserves, on the other hand, should be included; however, they are so small that we neglect them. We also neglect the role of coins which, unlike the banknotes, are not included in the redistribution mechanism and for which we have no database. Coins are a very small fraction of a country's monetary base.

The total amount of seignorage wealth that the 11 countries brought into the system as of January 1, 1999, was €352 billion. Naturally big countries contributed more than small countries. This is shown in figure 5.1, which relates a country's size to the seignorage wealth contributed.

We measure a country's size by the average of its shares in the aggregate GDP and in the aggregate population because, by the rules of the Maastricht Treaty, this average determines the share of the capital endowment contributed by that country. The ordinate of the diagram thus also measures this endowment. The total capital endowment is just €5 billion, which is tiny relative to the €352 billion stock of interest-bearing assets contributed in the form of seignorage wealth. A country's capital endowment has little more than a symbolic function and serves primarily to establish a stake in the seignorage profit.[7] It does not

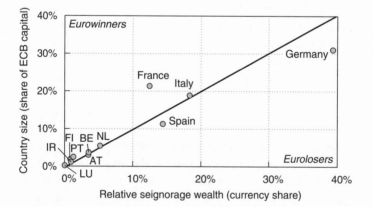

Figure 5.1
Country size and relative seignorage wealth. AT (Austria), BE (Belgium), FI (Finland), IR (Ireland), LU (Luxembourg), NL (Netherlands), PT (Portugal). The share of ECB capital is as of January 1, 1999; the currency share is as of December 31, 1998. (Sources: European Central Bank 1998—key for the ECB's capital, Press Release of December 1, Frankfurt; International Monetary Fund 2000—*International Financial Statistics*, March, Washington, DC)

involve any resource cost for the contributing countries, because the interest it generates for the ECB will be distributed in proportion to the capital endowment. The real contribution to the currency union is not the contribution to the equity capital but the contribution to the aggregate seignorage wealth—the interest-bearing assets that the national central banks had accumulated during their respective histories of money creation and whose return will be socialized. The share in the equity capital does not indicate a contribution but a drawing right—the right to participate in the profit distributions of the ECB. It determines the single country's share in the total seignorage wealth contributed by all countries.

Figure 5.1 shows that the correlation between the countries' shares in, and contributions to, seignorage wealth is close, but not perfect. Some countries, notably Spain and Germany, are located below the 45° line, others like France are located above that line. Germany contributes 39 percent and receives 31 percent of seignorage wealth, Italy contributes 18 percent and receives 19 percent, Spain contributes 14 percent and receives 11 percent, France contributes 12 percent and receives 21 percent. Obviously, as indicated in the introduction, there is considerable redistribution of seignorage wealth among the participating countries.

There are a number of reasons for the imbalance between country size and seignorage wealth. First of all, the German figure is so high not only because Germany is the largest country but also because the deutschmark was an important international transaction and reserve currency, taking second place to the dollar with a foreign circulation that is worth about €30–40 billion.[8] The fall of the iron curtain, the traditional strength of the German export industries, and the conservative monetary policy of the Bundesbank had all contributed to the dominant role of the deutschmark. The high figures for the Spanish seignorage wealth can partly be explained by the importance of the Spanish overseas connections, and partly by the large share of the Spanish shadow economy, where cash rather than bank transfers are used as a means of payment. According to Schneider and Ernste (2000) the Spanish share in GDP of black market activities is about 23 percent, while the figure for Germany is only 14 percent. The low share of seignorage wealth contributed by France may be attributed to the fact that the French franc was not used much outside that country, and possibly also to a well-developed banking sector and advanced payment habits.

5.4   Redistribution of Seignorage Wealth through EMU

The Maastricht Treaty mandates the ECB monetary income to be shared among member national central banks according to their respective capital key. If the capital keys happened to match the pre-euro distribution of seignorage wealth across the European countries, there would be no effective redistribution of seignorage wealth. In figure 5.1 all countries would be located strictly along the 45° line. However, this is not the case. For the reasons explained, a unit of capital carries very different amounts of seignorage wealth depending on where it comes from.

The exact implications for the redistribution of seignorage wealth are summarized in table 5.1, which refers to the situation of January 1, 1999. Columns one and two show the absolute and relative amounts of seignorage wealth contributed to the pool—the currency circulation— and columns three and four show the absolute and relative amounts of seignorage wealth received from the pool, where the latter is, as

Table 5.1
Winners and losers from the redistribution of seignorage wealth

	Seignorage wealth contributed		Seignorage wealth received		Gain or loss	
					Total:	€ Per
	€ Billion	Share	€ Billion	Share	€ billion	capita
	(1)	(2)	(3)	(4)	(5)	(6)
Austria	12.3	3.5%	10.5	3.0%	−1.8	−222
Belgium	12.5	3.6%	12.8	3.6%	+0.2	+24
Finland	3.0	0.8%	6.2	1.8%	+3.3	+634
France	43.8	12.4%	75.1	21.3%	+31.3	+535
Germany	138.6	39.4%	109.2	31.0%	−29.3	−358
Ireland	3.4	1.0%	3.8	1.1%	+0.4	+97
Italy	64.5	18.3%	66.4	18.9%	+1.9	+34
Luxembourg	0.1	0.0%	0.7	0.2%	+0.6	+1319
Netherlands	18.6	5.3%	19.1	5.4%	+0.5	+33
Portugal	4.6	1.3%	8.6	2.4%	+4.0	+401
Spain	50.7	14.4%	39.7	11.3%	−11.0	−281
Total	352.0	100.0%	352.0	100.0%	0.0	—

Sources: European Central Bank (1998)—key for the ECB's capital, Press Release, December 1, Frankfurt; International Monetary Fund (2000)—*International Financial Statistics*, March, Washington, DC; Statistisches Bundesamt (2000)—*Statistisches Jahrbuch für das Ausland*, Metzler-Poeschel, Stuttgart, p. 40.
Note: Share of ECB capital as of January 1, 1999; currency share and population data as of December 31, 1998.

explained, given by the shares of capital contributed which themselves reflect the population and GDP shares. The most interesting information is contained in columns 5 and 6. They show the absolute gains and losses of the different countries and the respective per capita amounts.

Clearly, France is the big winner and Germany the big loser of the redistribution of seignorage wealth. While France brings in €43.8 billion and receives €75.1 billion, Germany contributes €139 billion and receives €109 billion. The French gain is €31.3 billion, and the German loss is €29.3 billion. Without being aware of it, Germany made a net payment of about €30 billion to France to be able to participate in the currency union.

In per capita terms the redistribution between the two countries is also substantial. The average French citizen will gain €535, which corresponds to a sum of 3,510 francs, and the average German citizen will lose €358 or 699 deutschmarks.

Next to Germany, Spain is the largest loser. In total, the Spanish losses amount to €11.3 billion which is €281 or 46,761 pesetas per capita. Austria is the only further loser with €1.7 billion in total and €222 or 3,047 shillings per capita.

The majority of countries are winners: Portugal, Finland, Italy, Luxembourg, the Netherlands, Ireland, and Belgium, in the order of their absolute gains. A citizen of Luxembourg gains most, with €1,319 or 53,211 Belgian francs, followed by a Finn with €634 or 3,771 finmarks.[9]

To interpret these figures correctly, we repeat that they refer to the wealth equivalents of the redistribution of that part of the seignorage profit that can be attributed to the assets that the central banks had accumulated before January 1, 1999. There are two things that the reader should keep in mind in order not to misinterpret our results. First, the figures measure the once-and-for-all redistribution effect and do not refer to annual gains and losses. In principle, the annual gains and losses can be calculated by multiplying the figures given in column 5 of the table with a market rate of interest, but since it is not clear what the future rate will be, such a calculation would involve a good deal of guesswork. For the reasons explained, only a wealth-based calculation is free from such arbitrariness. Second, the redistribution figures include neither the present value of future increments in seignorage wealth that would have occurred in the course of a continued growth process had the euro not been introduced nor the present value of any additional future increments in seignorage wealth that might result

from a particular attractiveness of the euro as an international transactions and reserve currency (compare the introduction, categories 2
and 3). We do not want to argue that these increments should not be
distributed according to country size, but we want to raise the question
of whether the countries participating in the euro really wanted to
enact such a gigantic redistribution of claims on existing assets as they
have done.

5.5   Additional Participants to the Eurosystem

What happens as additional countries join the Eurosystem? In June 2000
Greece was accepted by the EU Council as a participant of the euro area
as of January 1, 2001. Did Greece gain or lose from participating in the
redistribution of historic seignorage wealth, and what did the Greek
participation cost the other countries? And what about Denmark, the
United Kingdom, and Sweden, should they ever wish to join? Have the
Danes missed the chance of becoming richer when they decided not to
join the EMU, or have they prevented a wealth loss by not joining?

The answers to these questions are given in table 5.2, which distin-
guishes alternative entrance scenarios. Columns 1 and 2 show how much
a country would gain if it were the only one to join the now-existing EMU.
Columns three and four refer to a certain entrance sequence and show

Table 5.2
Gains from participation in the euro system

	Single effect		Cumulative effect		All-inclusive effect	
	Total: € billion (1)	€ Per capita (2)	Total: € billion (3)	€ Per capita (4)	Total: € billion (5)	€ Per capita (6)
Greece	2.2	209	2.2	209	1.4	137
Denmark	2.8	524	2.7	515	2.2	409
United Kingdom	25.8	438	25.2	428	24.8	421
Sweden	3.8	434	2.9	330	2.9	330
Euro system	—	—	—	—	−31.3	−108

Sources: European Central Bank (1998)—key for the ECB's capital, Press Release,
December 1, Frankfurt; International Monetary Fund (2000)—*International Financial
Statistics*, March, Washington, DC; Statistisches Bundesamt (2000)—*Statistisches Jahrbuch
für das Ausland*, Metzler-Poeschel, Stuttgart, p. 40.
Note: Share of ECB capital as of January 1, 1999; monetary, exchange rate and population
data as of December 31, 1998.

how much a country would gain if it were the last to join after the countries listed above had already joined. For example, Sweden would gain €2.9 billion if it entered in addition to Greece, Denmark, and the United Kingdom and if no further country joined. Columns 5 and 6 finally show how much each single country would gain if all four candidates enter.

The table shows that all candidates for membership would indeed gain from a participation in the redistribution of historic seignorage wealth. If all countries join, the largest winner both in absolute and per capita terms will be the United Kingdom. It will be able to increase its claim on seignorage wealth by €25 billion, which is more than €400 per capita.

If Greece remains the only country to join the EMU, it will gain €2.2 billion in total, or €209 per capita. The decision to let Greece participate thus will not only provide this country with a stable currency but also with a considerable wealth endowment.

Had Denmark decided to join in addition to Greece while the United Kingdom and Sweden stayed absent, it would have gained another €2.7 billion in total, or €515 per capita. The per capita sum is one of the largest among the winning countries. One wonders whether the Danes have made a wise decision.

Of course, the gains depicted in table 5.2 are matched by equivalent losses of the now-existing 11 members in EMU. As we study the redistribution of a given stock of seignorage wealth, the sum of all gains and losses resulting from a new membership is zero. Table 5.3 clarifies how much individual countries that are now members of the euro system lose if additional countries join.

The first two columns show who pays how much for the Greek gain of €2.192 billion. Obviously Germany is again the largest payer with a net contribution of €680 million, which increases its total loss from the currency union to almost €30 billion. However, the French and Italian gains also shrink substantially by €467 million and €414 million, respectively. This sounds huge but in fact the respective per capita numbers are small. A German, French, or Italian citizen may well be prepared to pay the €7–8 which the Greek membership costs.

From a purely financial perspective, all countries should be happy that Denmark has decided not to join, for if it had done so, they would all have lost resources. Again, however, in per capita terms these are small numbers. Even a citizen of Luxembourg would not have lost more than €12.

Table 5.3
Losses due to the new participants

	Greece		Denmark		United Kingdom		Sweden	
	Total: € million (1)	€ Per capita (2)	Total: € million (3)	€ Per capita (4)	Total: € million (5)	€ Per capita (6)	Total: € million (7)	€ Per capita (8)
Austria	−66	−8.1	−79	−9.8	−720	−89.2	−71	−8.8
Belgium	−80	−7.8	−96	−9.5	−874	−85.9	−86	−8.4
Finland	−39	−7.6	−47	−9.1	−426	−83.0	−42	−8.2
France	−467	−8.0	−565	−9.7	−5134	−87.8	−505	−8.6
Germany	−680	−8.3	−822	−10.0	−7470	−91.1	−734	−9.0
Ireland	−24	−6.5	−29	−7.8	−259	−71.0	−25	−7.0
Italy	−414	−7.2	−500	−8.7	−4543	−79.1	−446	−7.8
Luxembourg	−4	−9.9	−5	−12.0	−46	−108.9	−4	−10.7
Netherlands	−119	−7.6	−144	−9.2	−1305	−83.8	−128	−8.2
Portugal	−53	−5.4	−65	−6.5	−587	−59.0	−58	−5.8
Spain	−247	−6.3	−299	−7.6	−2712	−69.0	−267	−6.8
Greece	+2192	+209.0	−69	−6.6	−627	−59.8	−62	−5.9
Denmark			+2719	+515.5	−510	−96.6	−50	−9.5
United Kingdom					+25211	+428.0	−440	−7.5
Sweden							+2917	+329.9

Sources: European Central Bank (1998)—key for the ECB's capital, Press Release, December 1, Frankfurt; International Monetary Fund (2000)—
International Financial Statistics, March, Washington, DC; Statistisches Bundesamt (2000)—*Statistisches Jahrbuch für das Ausland*, Metzler-Poeschel,
Stuttgart, p. 40.
Note: Share of ECB capital as of January 1, 1999; monetary, exchange rate, and population data as of December 31, 1998.

Most expensive would be the integration of the United Kingdom, which would cost Germany €7.5, France €5.1, and Italy €4.5 billion, respectively, and would impose a burden of between €80 and €90 on the citizens of most countries. Finally, if Sweden joined, the financial burden imposed on other countries would again be similar to that of Denmark.

5.6 How to Resolve the Problem

Given the magnitudes involved it is little wonder that calculations of this kind stirred up debates in 1997, especially in the losing countries.[10] As was mentioned in the introduction, the ECB reacted to this debate by postponing the redistributive arrangements laid down primarily in Article 32 of the Protocol on the Statute of the European System of Central Banks and of the ECB for a transition period of three years,[11] and then again for one more year since the introductory year of the euro, 2002, should be regarded as "special year" (ECB 2001, p. 55). Redistribution of seignorage would only take place on a large scale from January 1, 2003 onward, when the so-called earmarking method, which is reflected in the calculations presented here, became effective.

There is, however, a second transition period that is foreseen in Article 4 of a Decision of the European Central Bank of December 6, 2001, on the allocation of monetary income. By this article, an adjustment factor is defined that temporarily limits the redistribution. In the first year, only 14 percent of the seignorage resulting from banknotes in circulation is redistributed according to the capital keys. By 2007, this percentage will rise to 82 percent, and full socialization of historic seignorage wealth will be completed by January 1, 2008.

What can be done about the situation? Roesl and Schaefer (2000) argue that the central banks of the disadvantaged countries could be given the right to reduce their interest contributions to the pool by earmarking low-interest assets to their monetary bases. At first sight this seems to be a possible solution. However, the proposal neglects the fact that in EMU, a single country has little incentive to hold liquid, low-interest-bearing assets. If it holds such assets, it does so for the benefit of the whole system in terms of providing the necessary flexibility for open market operations. Suppose, starting from a situation where all countries hold high-interest assets, the ECB asks a particular central bank to exchange their assets against liquid low-interest assets in order to be able to gain more flexibility for market operations. This exchange reduces the interest income of the central bank and its interest contribution to the pool, while more liquidity services are available to the system. According to their size, all countries participate in the interest loss and in the liquidity services. A national gain, which could mitigate the disadvantages of the loser countries, will not result from this asset exchange.

Another suggestion was made by Sinn and Feist (1997) and supported by Gros (1998). Its essence was to allocate the *initial* equity contributions in proportion to the magnitudes of the respective monetary bases as of January 1, 1999, and the *additional* contributions necessitated by a future growth in the joint monetary base in proportion to country size. This suggestion implies that historic seignorage wealth is exempt from redistribution, although the increments in seignorage wealth due to the normal growth of the European economies and due to any extraordinary success of the euro are shared equally according to country size (see categories 2 and 3 of the introduction).

Such a rule would probably require an amendment to the Maastricht Treaty. Given that the redistribution clauses in the treaty were not understood by the signing parties, this amendment should be agreeable to the member countries.

Notes

1. The calculations presented in this chapter refer to wealth equivalents of long-term seignorage gains or losses, and not with the actual flows of transfers among the national central banks once EMU has begun. Predicting these flows would be meaningless since national moneys cease to exist. Given that with the euro, all central banks are able to produce the same quality of money, part of the German currency might well be issued in Portugal, and vice versa. This will affect the net flows of payments between the central banks but not the gains and losses calculated here, which are all measured relative to the situation without EMU.

2. Let i denote the common interest rate and r the common growth rate of the monetary base. Then the net gain or net loss of a country from category 2 is, in present value terms, $r/(i-r)$ times the respective figure calculated for category 1, whatever that may be. If, say, $r = 4$ percent and $i = 6$ percent, then the factor is 2; that is, the net gain or loss from categories 1 and 2 taken together is three times the figure we report in this article. This was pointed out by Wenger (1997) in a response to Sinn (1997).

3. In monetary theory, seignorage wealth is even considered as net wealth for the whole economy, because the currency generates private liquidity services that outweigh the interest forgone by holding it.

4. In addition the liquidity services of low-interest assets would have to be considered.

5. The present value of an income stream is defined as today's market value of an asset that is able to generate this stream. Thus the equivalence between our stock approach and a correctly specified flow approach holds strictly, regardless of what the time paths of

returns on the assets earmarked to back the currency will be, provided that the assets backing the currency are evaluated at their true market prices.

6. While France only imposed an interest-free minimum reserve requirement of between 0.5 and 1 percent on its banks, and countries like Greece, Italy, Ireland, and the Netherlands paid interest on the minimum reserves held by the private banking system, Germany had a rather restrictive system. From 1950 to 1994 the Bundesbank required that well over 10 percent of a bank's demand deposits be backed by central bank money without paying interest for it. Sinn and Feist (1997) therefore studied the implication of alternative harmonisation scenarios for the distribution of seignorage wealth.

7. Not even the countries' voting power in the ECB Governing Council depends on it. While Germany, for example, brings in 39 percent of seignorage wealth and has a capital share of 31 percent, its share of votes is 9 percent.

8. See Rogoff (1998) and Seitz (1995).

9. Although our results are based on the superior knowledge enabled by hindsight, they are closely in line with our earlier projections published in Sinn and Feist (1997).

10. The political interest in the redistribution of seignorage wealth is well documented in a query in the German parliament (Deutscher Bundestag 1997), in which the secretary of state at the ministry of finance reports that the Bundesbank will stress the point in further consultations with EU central banks and urge for a strengthening of the German position.

11. Instead of the arrangements described in the Protocol, an auxiliary redistribution method was agreed on for the transition period. According to this method, the monetary income to be distributed among the central banks is determined indirectly (hence the term "indirect method") by simply multiplying a specified reference rate of interest with a defined liability base of the ECB. The reference rate of interest is equal to the interest rate of main refinancing operations, and the defined liability base consists of current accounts, deposit facilities, fixed term deposits, fine-tuning reserve operations and deposits related to margin calls. The assets backing the banknotes in circulation were deliberately excluded from the liability base in order to postpone the effective redistribution mechanism. For a similar reason, interest paid by national central banks on items within the liability base is deductible and only the net income is pooled. Since minimum reserve requirement deposits that constitute the bulk of the so-defined liability base are remunerated at the euro system's main refinancing rate, the order of magnitude of the income eligible for redistribution turned out to be very small (about €35 million). In fact the income calculated this way was not even enough to cover the ECB's operating cost such that, in 1999, the ECB had to charge its member banks a fee of €184.6 million in total (European Central Bank 2000).

References

Deutsche Bundesbank. 2000. *Protokoll der Pressekonferenz im Anschluß an die Zentralbankratssitzung der Deutschen Bundesbank am 6. April*, Frankfurt.

Deutscher Bundestag. 1997. Verringerung der Bundesbankgewinne ab Beginn der dritten Stufe der Europäischen Wirtschafts- und Währungsunion. *Fragen und Antworten für die Fragestunde*. Drucksache13/8310. Berlin, pp. 13–14.

European Central Bank. 2001. Decision of the European Central Bank of 6 December 2001 on the allocation of monetary income of the national central banks of participating member states from the financial year 2002. *Official Journal of the European Communities* (ECB/2001/16), December 20, 2001, pp. 55–58.

European Central Bank. 2000. *Annual Accounts of the ECB for the Year Ended 31 December 1999.* Press Release, Frankfurt.

Gros, D. 1998. Distributing Seignorage under EMU. *Ifo Schnelldienst,* no. 17–18, 29–39.

Remsperger, H. 1996. Umverteilung der Notenbenkgewinne in der Währungsunion. Milliardenverluste für den Bundeshaushalt? *Wirtschaftsdienst der BHF-Bank,* no. 181: 1–3.

Roesl, G., and W. Schaefer. 2000. A conceptual approach to the creation and allocation of central bank profits in the euro area. *Kredit und Kapital* 33: 39–61.

Rogoff, K. 1998. Blessing or curse? Foreign and underground demand for euro notes. *Economic Policy* 28: 261–303.

Schneider, F., and D. H. Ernste. 2000. Shadow economies: Size, causes, and consequences. *Journal of Economic Literature* 38: 77–114.

Seitz, F. 1995. Der DM-Umlauf im Ausland, Volkswirtschaftliche Forschungsgruppe der Deutschen Bundesbank. *Bundesbank Diskussionspapier* 1/95.

Sinn, H.-W. 1997. Der Euro kostet Deutschland bis zu 90 Milliarden DM. *Frankfurter Allgemeine Zeitung,* no. 127 (June 5): 17.

Sinn, H.-W., and H. Feist. 1997. Eurowinners and eurolosers: The distribution of seignorage wealth in EMU. *European Journal of Political Economy* 13: 665–89.

Wenger, E. 1997. Nicht 90, sondern 150 Milliarden Verlust durch den Euro. *Frankurter Allgemeine Zeitung,* no. 141 (July 21): 12.

Comment on Chapter 5

Jouko Vilmunen

I do not, and actually cannot, dispute Sinn and Feist's basic observation that there will be a redistribution of seignorage wealth across EMU countries. What I do not find plausible is the assumption of accidentality, or even the windfall nature of the ensuing distribution, an assumption that underlies most of their conclusions and suggestions on approaches to compensate, apparently, the eurolosers for the losses due to the (accidental) redistribution of seignorage wealth. However, before I present my objections and criticism of their analysis and conclusions, let me quickly review the nature of the problem.

The Problem

The following summarizes the sequence of main arguments put forward in chapter 5:

• By and large, a country's seignorage wealth is equal to its monetary base, which is then its contribution to the aggregate seignorage wealth in the EMU.

• The Maastricht Treaty mandates the ECB monetary income to be shared among the member central banks according to their capital keys, that is, according to the shares dictated by the average of the size of the population and GDP relative to the corresponding EU-wide aggregates.

• Capital keys do not match the pre-euro distribution of seignorage wealth: discrepancy between contributions to seignorage wealth and distributive shares as implied by the capital keys.

• Redistribution of seignorage wealth will as a result take place.

• The implied redistribution of the seignorage wealth was not part of the bargain at the time the Treaty was signed.

- Hence this redistribution should not be accepted.

- Something should be done to undo the discrepancy.

- Rewrite the Treaty? Apply an adjustment period prior to using the mandated capital keys in full? Something else?

Some Questions and Comments

The analysis and, in particular, the conclusions based on the analysis, raises some questions and comments. Since the analysis in the chapter does not delve too deeply into economic-theoretic grounds, just to save space and time, I will simply list these.

- The numbers and calculations given in the chapter—and in the earlier 1997 EJPE paper[1]—can hardly be disputed. A minor comment relates to tax base versus tax rate. Observed pre-euro differences in the monetary base among the member countries clearly mean that as far as seignorage revenue is concerned, quantitatively important differences among the member countries exist in terms of the size of the relevant tax base. To this end the contribution provides a systematic analysis of redistribution from differences in the relevant country-specific tax bases. For differences in seignorage revenue, differences in cross-country tax rates (inflation rates) also matter. To me, the calculations in the chapter abstract from these differences. However, these differences are quite likely to be small (i.e., of second-order magnitude).

- How should we interpret the differences in the tax bases? What do they reflect? How are differences in central bank's (policy) objectives, the role of the central bank in a country's payment system, and the size of its monetary base linked? Systematic analysis of the efficiency of payment systems and their relation to the size of the base should have complemented the analysis of the chapter.

- The 1997 paper gives the most benign interpretation of why, in particular, the German monetary base is so sizable: the DM's role as an international currency (largely an outcome of successful and credible monetary policy in Germany). This certainly is an important factor, but is it the only one? Can't we argue that Buba has had a strong bias in favor of a payment system (mainly) based on the use of money—notes (and coins)? For example, doesn't having had a high reserve requirement reflect this bias? Also, what is the ultimate weight of the argument that the DM is an important international currency, since most of the

DMs outside Germany fuel many of the economies in the former socialist camp (Russia, in particular).

• In the case of Spain—another quantitatively important euroloser— the chapter offers an explanation in terms of the shadow economy and inefficient payment/banking system. It is evidently true that the size of the shadow economy in Spain is larger than in Germany, as is noted. But are these differences large enough to sustain the claim that the monetary base is sizable in Spain mainly because of the size of the shadow economy and inefficent banking system? Furthermore, what about inefficiencies in the payment/banking system in Germany (size of banks, technological sophistication of the banking sector and payment system, etc.)?

• I would like to argue that deliberate policy choices to favor money could have affected the size of the monetary base in high-base countries like Austria and Germany.

• If deliberate policy choices have played a role, can we really convincingly argue that countries participating in the euro did not, at the time they made the decision to participate, know that even sizable redistribution may lie ahead? Particularly when the existing differences and asymmetries in the structure of the banking systems, money markets, and so forth, were well known? I do not find Sinn and Feist's claim that those making the decisions were not informed of the future redistribution plausible. Especially I find the arguments of accidentality, or even windfall nature, of the redistribution weak. At the time of making the decisions to enter, the existing amount of research, analysis and discussions (also) over the differences in cross-country monetary bases was sufficiently large to warrant the opposite claim that the redistributional implications were understood. I can't escape the conclusions that the eurolosers were willing the pay the price (in terms of lost seignorage wealth) for the membership, or, more interestingly (realistically?), for not to risk the joint European venture. All in all, to me the issue of redistribution of seignorage wealth was not high on the political agenda at the time of the decision making.[2]

• One could argue that economic arguments are, in the end, weak when resolving perceived problems related to redistribution of wealth. Basically the arguments are complex excercises in political bargaining. If, then, we do not want to stick to the view that "since you signed the agreement, you should respect it; today there is thus no problem to be solved," what alternative could we entertain? Rewriting the Treaty?

Applying the capital keys fully only after a number of years (historic seignorage wealth exempt from redistribution)?

• Rewriting the Treaty should be ruled out categorically! The reason is that there is the risk of introducing a precedence. Also, strictly speaking, applying different capital keys that the Treaty dictates means, in effect, deviating from the Treaty (i.e., to change it), which has to be accepted by the member countries. Once again, this procedure, although possibly politically the most feasible one, opens up the possibility for precedence, as could be used subsequently in similar situations involving political sensitivities.

• For me there is an economically sensible and effective way of solving the problem. This involves the heads of state getting together to decide over (voluntary) monetary transfers from the eurowinners to the eurolosers. Economically, at least, this appears to be way out. Politically it may be more difficult, since it involves the possibility of the division of the cake, namely a price for these transfers that the euro losers might have to pay.

All in all, I think that rewriting the opening of the Treaty is the wrong approach. This is because there is the danger of introducing more distributive conflicts in the future as differences arise in the member countries' other, more conventional, tax bases. Do we wait until we have a common fiscal agent serving multiple national fiscal principals to see the power of the precedence created by rewriting the Treaty now?

Notes

1. Sinn, H.-W. and Feist, H. 1997. Eurowinners and eurolosers; the distribution of seignorage wealth in EMU. *European Journal of Political Economy* 4(4): 665–89.

2. For example, in commenting on the estimated distribution of seignorage wealth among the community countries (p. 675), the authors first note that France and the United Kingdom are the two big winners. Then they add a comment that "The sum of these two gains would be enough to build another three tunnels underneath the Channel"!

6   Financial Fragility, Bubbles, and Monetary Policy

Gerhard Illing

Mr. Greenspan's confidence that he can use monetary policy to prevent a deep recession if share prices crash exposes an awkward asymmetry in the way central banks respond to asset prices. They are reluctant to raise interest rates to prevent a bubble, but they are quick to cut rates if financial markets tremble. Last autumn, in the wake of Russia's default and a slide in share prices, the Fed swiftly cut rates, saying it wanted to prevent a credit crunch. As a result, share prices soared to new highs. The Fed has inadvertently created a sort of moral hazard. If investors believe that monetary policy will underpin share prices, they will take bigger risks.
Economist, September 25, 1999

6.1 Introduction

The past decade has been characterized by a steady and sustained decline of inflation rates to an unprecedented low level. At the same time, however, there has been a dramatic surge in asset prices, followed by increasing volatility. Many economists consider at least part of this rise as a bubble with possibly damaging effects, with monetary policy itself as one factor responsible for generating bubbles.

In the United States, for a long time, monetary policy paid attention to movements in stock prices. Alan Greenspan has frequently been blamed for having contributed to a bubble in the US stock markets by reacting asymmetrically to movements in stock prices (compare the quote above). Both in 1987 and during the crisis triggered by the collapse of the hedge fund Long-Term Capital Management (LTCM) in 1998, the Fed eased monetary policy fast, aiming to prevent a credit crunch, whereas it did not react to dampen the boom on the stock market or even try to prick a supposed bubble. This asymmetry, it is argued, gives investors the feeling that monetary policy works like a put option on the stock index, encouraging quasi-rational exuberance (see Miller, Weller, and Zhang 2002): Being confident that monetary policy will bail them out in a crash, investors feel safe to put their funds in more risky assets, thus creating a bubble. The central objective of this chapter is to analyze to what extent such central bank behavior might be rationalized and to assess its consequences.

6.1.1 Banking versus Securitization—A Brief Survey of the Financial Structure in the Euro Area

Whereas in the United States, movements in stock prices are considered to be an important factor for predicting monetary policy, the stock market has been of much less concern in the euro area in the past. One reason for this may be the sharp differences in financial structure between the two economies. In the euro area, bank loans are the dominating source of finance. In Germany loans represent 50 percent of nonfinancial companies' liabilities, whereas securitized liabilities (equity and bonds) have a share of less than 20 percent (see figure 6.1). In remarkable contrast, with a share of 72.2 percent they are the dominating source of finance in the United States (the share of banking being just 15 percent, compare also figure 6.2). In the United States institutional investors take the role played by banks in the euro area, as pointed out by Davis (2000). What are the consequences of these differences? First, in an economy with a

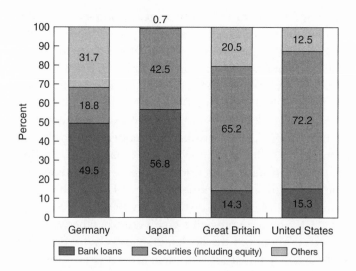

Figure 6.1
Components of nonfinancial companies' intersectoral liabilities, percentage of total liabilities at market prices. (Source: Hackethal and Schmidt 2000)

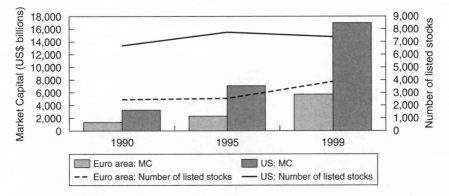
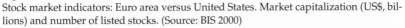

Figure 6.2
Stock market indicators: Euro area versus United States. Market capitalization (US$, billions) and number of listed stocks. (Source: BIS 2000)

small part of financial wealth in the form of equity, wealth effects of stock prices (a controversial issue even in the United States, see Bernanke and Gertler 1999) should not have a significant impact on the transmission mechanism. Second, balance sheet effects—the most prominent propagator of asset price changes to the real economy—may loose part of their impact, since a financial system with relationship lending may reduce the amount of asymmetric information central to these phenomena. For similar reasons exposure to systemic risk arising from a collapse of asset prices used to be much lower in the euro area.

In this chapter we argue that convergence in financial structure between the United States and the euro area may change this pattern in monetary policy making. Surprisingly, and contrary to conventional wisdom, there has been no major evidence for such a trend during the past decade. In their detailed empirical analysis Schmidt, Hackethal, and Tyrell (1997) found in Germany no general trend toward disintermediation or toward a transformation from bank-based to capital market-based financial systems, nor a loss of importance of banks (compare also figures 6.3 and 6.4). During recent years, however, signs of a significant change point to an end of the quiet times in euroland. Equities and—to a lesser extent—bonds become more important both as means of external finance (figure 6.4) and as component of financial wealth (figure 6.3).

Although the identification of such trends is complicated due to intra-European divergences and lack of consistent data (so figures 6.3

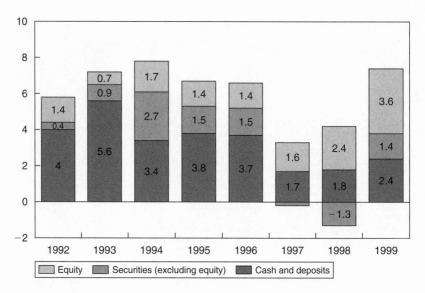

Figure 6.3
EMU: Selected components of investment of private nonfinancial sectors, percentage of
GDP. (Source: ECB, October 2000)

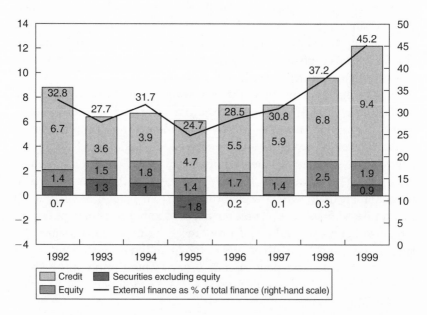

Figure 6.4
EMU: Selected components of external financing of nonfinancial sectors, percentage of
GDP. (Source: ECB, October 2000)

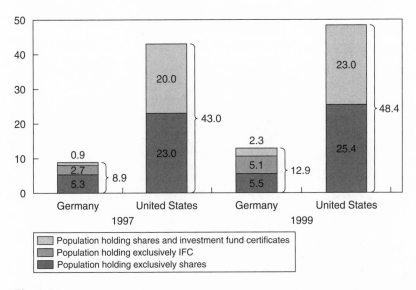

Figure 6.5
Shareholders in Germany and in the United States, percentage of total population. The data for the United States includes individuals exclusively holding shares. (Source: Deutsches Aktieninstitut)

and 6.4 have to be handled with care), we see major signs pointing in this direction. In Germany, for example, the IPO of Deutsche TeleKom end of 1996 and the opening of the new market in March 1997 gave a big push to share holding (see figure 6.5). Certainly still much lower than in the United States, the percentage of individuals holding shares doubled from 8.9 percent in 1997 to 17.7 percent in 2000. As shown in figure 6.6, this rise is mainly due to equities held in the form of investment fund certificates. Together with the strong growth both in market capitalization and in the number of listed stocks (figure 6.2), this evidence suggests an increasing role for equity markets as part of the financial system. It is also supported by some micro trends, such as the increase in venture capital finance in the euro area, as pointed out by the *Bundesbank* (Monthly Bulletin, October 2000).

Developments in the market for corporate bonds are somewhat less clear-cut. Since the start of the new currency, issues in euro (as compared to its predecessor currencies) have reached long-time highs, admittedly starting from an extremely low level. As noted in this years *BIS Annual Report* (2000, p. 129), "the composition of borrowers that have tapped the euro bond market partly reflects the traditional structure of

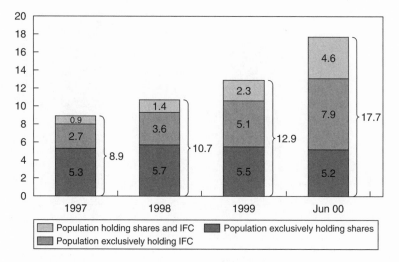

Figure 6.6
Shareholders in Germany, percentage of total population. (Source: Deutsches Aktieninstitut)

European finance, but partly also its changing profile." Compared to issues by European banks, the share of bonds issued by nonfinancial corporations is still small, but growing. The telecommunications sector plays a key role. It financed large parts of its huge investments through bond issues, contributing to a concentration of credit risk in this sector.

Starting from the observation of probably converging, but still heterogeneous financial market structures, one may suspect that asset prices should follow distinct patterns in the United States and Euroland. But co-movements of stock prices in the two areas are a stylized fact of international equity markets. In particular, shares of new-economy firms experienced unusually large price increases in both markets (see figure 6.7). Contrary to conventional wisdom, at some stage price hikes of shares listed in the German Nemax index became even more pronounced than those in Nasdaq. These hikes were followed by equally pronounced collapses in recent months. It thus seems that both economies experienced swings in share prices of a possibly damaging magnitude (figures 6.7 and 6.8).

Such volatility may have damaging effects if the economy (i.e., borrowers and financial institutions) is sufficiently exposed to asset price risk. Although marginal investors in new economy shares experienced large losses in recent months (figure 6.7), the real economy does not

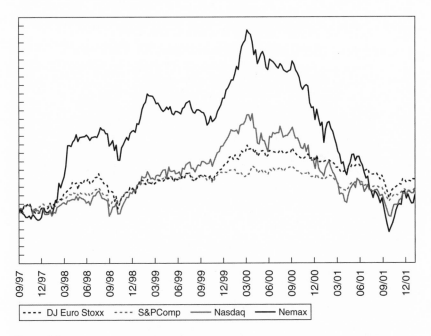

Figure 6.7
Share prices in Europe and the United States. Log of indexes, 01/09/97 = 100. (Source: Datastream)

seem to be hit until now. So exposure to asset price risk does not seem to be of much concern. We argue that such reasoning may be premature. Take the telecommunication sector, which provides a perfect example for the theoretical analysis of this chapter. Recent doubts whether telecom firms will be able to generate sufficient cash flows to justify highly leveraged investments and high share prices (figure 6.8) already had an impact on financial stability. In the United States, they contributed to the recent drying out of the high-yield bond market. In Europe, several regulatory institutions expressed concerns about overexposure of banks to this sector.

Real estate is another market where highly leveraged transactions are a common phenomenon. Not only the experience of Japan shows that policy makers should pay special attention to this sector. Although some urban areas in the United States experienced exceptionally large increases since 1995, there are no signs of a pronounced bubble for commercial or residential property in the US market. The same holds true for Europe on an aggregate level. Here the biggest markets are only

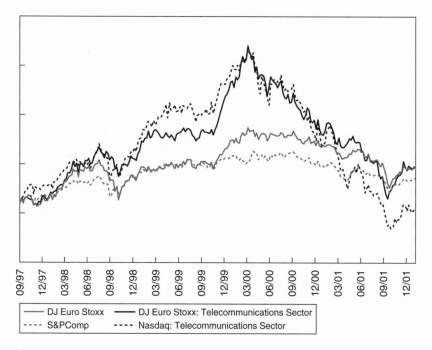

Figure 6.8
Share prices of telecom firms in Europe and the United States. Log of indexes, 01/09/97 = 100. (Source: Datastream)

starting to recover from times of oversupply since the late 1980s. However, on a national level, countries like Ireland or the Netherlands already show signs of overheating, manifesting themselves in fast credit growth and exploding prices, and indicating the need for a close monitoring by the monetary authority (see figure 6.9 for an overview).

The ECB has to be prepared to the trends outlined above. The increasing importance of securatized liabilities, especially shares, and rising volatility in asset markets in fact already have affected monitoring activities, as evidenced by a recent ECB (2000) study of asset prices and banking stability. But monitoring may not be enough. In the future the ECB (as well as other central banks) will have to answer questions about the role asset prices should play in formulating monetary policy.

6.1.2 Monetary Policy and Asset Prices
The striking contrast between price stability for consumer goods and "inflation" of asset prices has recently stimulated research in the role of

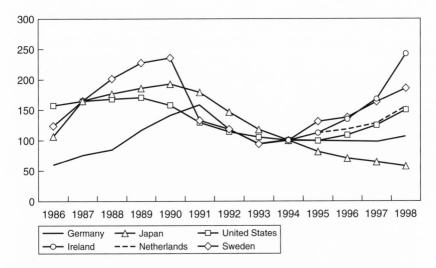

Figure 6.9
Commercial real estate prices for selected countries (major cities). Indexes, 1994 = 100.
(Source: ECB, May 2000)

asset prices for monetary policy. Two issues are at the center of the discussion:

1. Are rising asset prices a useful predictor for future inflation? Might stronger attention to asset price movements contribute to price stability by improving the performance of inflation forecasts? According to conventional wisdom, central banks should—and do—pay attention to asset prices only to the extent that they are an indicator for inflationary pressure. Recently, however, a CEPR report by Cecchetti et al. (2000) has strongly argued that asset prices should be included in the Taylor-rule as a separate element. As long as asset prices are treated as forward-looking variables and provide reliable information,[1] including them in a reaction function is likely to improve performance relative to a traditional, backward-looking Taylor rule. This is mainly an empirical issue: Starting with Bernanke and Gertler (1999), a number of papers simulated the performance of various reaction functions for an economy exposed to a stochastic bubble. So far, however, the evidence is rather mixed. The precise functional specification used determines, whether inclusion of asset prices helps to improve the performance (compare Bernanke and Gertler 1999; Cecchetti et al. 2000; Batini and Nelson 2000).

2. Does monetary policy itself contribute to the creation of bubbles? Central banks are expected to provide liquidity in order to prevent financial instability triggered by a crash on stock markets. Investors that anticipate an asymmetric response may be encouraged to overinvest in risky activities.

The Cecchetti-CEPR report proposes to avoid this asymmetry by including asset prices explicitly in a modified Taylor rule. Since such a rule would commit central banks to respond symmetrically to asset price movements, it would—so they claim—tackle both issues discussed at the same time. By dampening asset price misalignments, such misalignments would be less likely to occur right from the beginning, and their magnitude would be likely to be smaller. This suggestion is not convincing for at least two reasons. First, the optimal response crucially depends on the nature of the shock causing movements in asset prices. So it can never be optimal to bind the central bank to a mechanical rule, committing it to respond in a predetermined symmetric way to changes in asset prices. Evidently efficient policy requires a careful analysis of the specific type of shocks underlying any price change. Quarrels about the extent of misalignments leave plenty of room for discretionary arguments.[2]

Second, in the approach used by Cecchetti et al. (2000), one key reason for the supposed asymmetric response is not modeled at all: concerns about financial stability, which are at the center of the argument, are not included. The authors simulate the effect of a bubble in a Bernanke and Gertler type dynamic new Keynesian model with financial accelerator effects. As already pointed out by Dornbusch (1999), the structure of this model focuses exclusively on variations in risk premia and so misses a crucial element of the story—the risk of a breakdown of the whole system arising from financial fragility:[3] "once markets crash, . . . markets plain stop in terms of flow and rollovers and, thus, within a short period, risk inducing pervasive default. Here, big rate cuts and housing markets with cheap credit, not many questions asked are essential" (Dornbusch 1999, p. 133).

This chapter aims to shed light on exactly this aspect. In a crisis the central bank's policy objective is to prevent the disruption of financial intermediation. The central bank is not concerned with preventing stock market crashes as an end in itself. Obviously the policy response will depend on the financial structure of the economy, and so there is a need to model explicitly the degree of financial fragility. Since a crucial element for any analysis of central bank's reaction to crashes is the exposure of the whole economy to financial fragility, this chapter models explicitly the link between financial fragility and monetary policy. This requires a set up mixing elements of micro and macro analysis.

6.1.3   Outline of the Chapter and Related Literature

We consider an economy with two sectors. Investment in the old economy sector is safe, whereas investment in the other sector, the new economy, is risky. Given the observational equivalence between the bursting of a bubble and bad news about real shocks, usually it is extremely hard (except for the model builder) to identify the existence of a bubble even ex post. Rather than assuming that pure bubbles may burst with some exogenous probability, we model a crash as a rational response to bad news about profitability of firms in the new economy sector. Following Allen and Gale (2000), we define "bubbles" in the following precise sense: Due to overinvestment in the risky sector, the asset price in that sector—the rent of the scarce resources—is driven up above its fundamental value. So the bubble is modeled as the distortion of the relative price of an asset.

As the key factor for monetary policy actions, we single out financial fragility. As long as equity is the main source of finance for risky activities, leverage effects are small, so risk of disruption is low. In that case there is no need for monetary policy intervention when the stock market crashes, since there is no risk of early liquidation and disruption of the whole economy.

In contrast, with a highly leveraged financial structure, characterized by high debt exposure to intermediaries, a crash triggers a "run" on intermediaries, resulting in the disruption of intermediation and costly early liquidation of real assets in the absence of central bank intervention. The central bank is concerned about the destruction of the information capital that is specific to the banking sector (the expertise gained from relationship-lending). By providing sufficient liquidity, monetary policy can prevent disruption of intermediation, thus enabling the restructuring of solvent, but illiquid firms (compare the policy during the LTCM crisis vs. the policy in Japan beginning of the 1990s).

Since inflation reduces the real value of nominal debt, the surviving firms enjoy capital gains. Investors rationally anticipate these capital gains. This drives up the asset price above the fundamental value, thus creating a bubble equal to the expected value of capital gains out of central bank's rescue operations. The bubble is equal to the expected value of capital gains on outstanding debt.

A variety of economic mechanisms may create a bubble. In this chapter we consider three mechanisms: (1) irrational exuberance of investors, (2) weak financial intermediation (weak monitoring may allow investors to appropriate the gains out of risky investment and shift part of the losses to the financial sector), and (3) the central bank's concern about financial stability as a kind of put option for risky activities.[4] The first two effects have been documented extensively in the literature. Section 6.2 briefly illustrates both effects within a simple model. First, we characterize the fundamental value of the asset and then demonstrate how irrational exuberance and weak monitoring may create bubbles. Since financial stability issues are not essential for these two cases, we abstract from liquidation costs in order to analyze the issue in the most simple setup. The model is related to the work of Allen and Gale (2000a), as we present a short version of their approach.

From this starting point, in section 6.3, in the core part of the chapter, we analyze the impact of the central bank's concern about financial stability. This role of the bank is currently a hot issue among central bankers and financial market participants, but as far as we know, it has not yet been modeled explicitly. The reason is that no tractable framework has been available up to now for analyzing this role. We present a very simple, stylized model illustrating conditions under which monetary policy may create a bubble and analyze the rationality behind such a policy.

The risk of a run triggering inefficient liquidation of projects plays a key role for financial stability. Following Allen and Gale (2000b), we introduce aggregate risk into the standard Diamond and Dybvig bank run model: as the new economy is confronted by an aggregate shock, depositors run the banks, and all projects are liquidated unless the central bank provides sufficient liquidity. Our approach is closely related to work by Allen and Gale, but we will model the mechanisms by which monetary policy may create bubbles. In particular, we will analyze the central bank's trade-offs with such policy. In so doing, we characterize the costs and benefits of central bank's rescue operations.

6.2   Bubble-Creating Mechanisms

6.2.1   The Basic Model
The set up of the model is a modified and drastically simplified version of Allen and Gale (2000a). There are two sectors. Investment in the old technology sector Y is assumed to be riskless. Investment in the safe sector yields a safe gross return $1 + r$.

In the new economy sector X, investment is risky—when projects turn out to be successful (with probability q), they yield a high return R. But (with probability $1 - q$), they also run the risk of failure. In case of failure the return is low $C < 1 + r < R$.[5]

To simplify, the supply of risky projects is assumed to be fixed. It should be interpreted as the (short-run) inelastic supply of scarce skills in human wealth, of those being capable to design new economy projects (innovators with entrepreneurial spirits but lacking the capital to found start up firms). (Alternatively, the fixed asset may be viewed as land, modeling bubbles in land prices). Whereas each innovator has a measure of 0, the aggregate supply of new economy projects has measure 1.

In the economy there are four types of agents: (1) The innovators supply risky projects for the new economy. (2) Venture capitalists own funds E that they can either use as equity in the new economy or for investment in the old economy. Since they have the specific knowledge to evaluate projects in the new economy, they can fund these projects as venture capitalists in start-up firms. (3) Depositors who are willing to invest their wealth W for future consumption supply these funds inelastically. They do not, however, have the expertise to act as venture capitalists, and they so can invest only via deposits at banks. (4) Investments of the depositors is channeled to the firms via a competitive banking industry. Both banks and venture capitalists are assumed to be risk neutral.

The price of the risky asset is P_X. The aggregate supply of funds is $W + E$. Since the availability of the risky asset is normalized to $X = 1$, the aggregate constraint on investment and saving is

$$Y + P_X X = Y + P_X = W + E.$$

Under full information, in the absence of distortions, the asset price is equal to the present value of expected returns. An asset price bubble occurs whenever the market price exceeds this fundamental value. The bubble has distortionary effects on the economy: the higher the asset price of the risky sector, the lower the funds available to be invested in the old economy sector, thus reducing aggregate production.

Since the supply of new economy projects is assumed to be fixed in the short run, the distortion here manifests itself as a pure rent captured by the innovators: the bubble redistributes resources toward these innovators. Using a utilitarian approach, behind the veil of ignorance (at a stage before agents know whether they will be innovators, venture capitalists or depositors), the welfare-maximizing rent is equal to the present value of expected returns; any deviation from this price causes distortions.[6]

6.2.2 The Fundamental Value of the Asset

As a reference point, we first consider the allocation in the case of perfect financial markets. Let us assume initially that investment in the risky sector is purely equity financed. For each unit invested, the gross return is $[qR + (1 - q)C]/P_X$. So in equilibrium, the following arbitrage equation must hold:

$$1 + r = \frac{qR + (1 - q)C}{P_X}.$$

The asset price is equal to the discounted expected present value of the risky asset:

$$P_X^* = \frac{qR + (1 - q)C}{1 + r},$$

where P_X^* is the fundamental value of the asset. As illustrated below, in an economy with efficient intermediation the asset is priced at this value.

6.2.3 Irrational Exuberance

When investors are overconfident, their subjective perception of future returns of the asset will be upward biased. Whereas, for a long time, it used to be unpopular to blame bubbles on pure irrationality, behavioral finance recently gave a variety of sound scientific motivations for this phenomenon. In the setup here, all of these stories can essentially be captured by the subjective overestimation either of the good return R or of the success probability q. An overestimation $\hat{R} > R$ creates the following bubble:

$$P_{\hat{X}} = \frac{q\hat{R} + (1 - q)C}{1 + r} > P_X^* \quad \text{with} \quad P_{\hat{X}} - P_X^* = \frac{q(\hat{R} - R)}{1 + r}.$$

Recent research provides sophisticated arguments for this phenomenon, such as the herding behavior of institutional investors. With heterogeneous agents (some being less overconfident), the absence of short sales is a crucial condition to prevent realization of arbitrage possibilities. A serious shortcoming of this way to explain bubbles is the observational equivalence between overconfidence and favorable new information: good news about the profitability of the new economy sector will lead to a revision of forecasts about the investment return. The asset price is exactly the same as in the bubble characterized above, if forecasts are revised upward by $\hat{R} - R$. Ex post, once an aggregate crash has occurred, there is no way to distinguish between these two explanations.

6.2.4 Real Bubbles Arising from Weak Financial Intermediation

Above we saw that the asset price is determined by the expected present value when investment is financed by equity, unless there is overconfidence among investors. In general, however, investors do not have enough equity and need credit to finance investment in the new technology. In this section, for simplification (without loss of generality), we consider only the (interesting) case where the return in the bad state is not sufficient to cover gross debt payments $C < (1 + r)(P_X - E)$, so investors will be bankrupt when the project fails. C can be seen as the collateral investors are able to pledge to the bank.

Obviously credit contracts may give investors an incentive for risk shifting to the financial sector, making use of the leverage effect. So financial intermediaries are facing a monitoring problem: the lower the equity share of investors, the higher the risk for the bank. Allen and Gale (2000a) have shown that weak financial intermediation can create a "real bubble." They assume that banks are not able to monitor how investors allocate their funds across the two sectors. This gives investors a strong incentive for excess investment in the risky sector. As a result of the monitoring problem, the asset price is driven above its fundamental value.

In this section we illustrate the effects in an extremely stylized version of the Allen-Gale model, highlighting the economic mechanism behind. While in their model investors are assumed to have no own funds, we allow for equity of investors and show that the bubble occurs as long as equity plus collateral is less than the fundamental value of the asset. The bubble is a direct implication of the leverage effect of credit finance. In the two-state version of the model presented here, this can be illustrated in a straightforward, intuitive way: under credit finance, when intermediaries cannot monitor investment, the asset price is driven up to the present value of returns in the good state.

As the most drastic example of inefficient monitoring, let us now assume that banks cannot condition lending on the share of equity invested in the new economy sector. They cannot observe in which sector investors put their funds and are not able to claim investor's equity invested outside of the project. Again, the own rate of return for investors must be equal across both sectors. With credit finance, return to the investor increases with increasing credit finance as a consequence of the leverage effect:

$$qR + (1 - q)C - q(1 + r)[P_X - E] - (1 - q)C = (1 + r)E.$$

Monitoring problems drive up the asset price P_X (the rent to the scarce resource) to

$$P_X = \frac{R}{1+r} - \frac{1-q}{q}E,$$

$$P_X > P_X^* \quad \text{for} \quad \frac{q(R-C)}{1+r} > E.$$

Using the definition of P_X^*, this condition is equivalent to $P_X^* > [C/(1+r)] + E$. There is a bubble whenever outside finance is needed—that is, investor's equity plus the present value of the collateral C, which can be pledged, is not sufficient to cover the fundamental value. Because of the monitoring problems, banks are not able to make claims on the investor's equity invested in the old economy sector. Thus, whenever investors apply for outside funds, it will always be optimal for them to put all own funds in the old economy. Investment in the new economy is then financed purely via credit—so as to make best use of the leverage effect. Consequently no equity finance will be used for investment in the new economy. With $E = 0$, the asset price is driven up to

$$P_X = \frac{R}{1+r},$$

where P_X is equal to the present value in case the project turns out to be successful, since investors care only for that case. The bubble component amounts to

$$P_X - P_X^* = \frac{(1-q)(R-C)}{1+r}.$$

It is straightforward to see that the bubble is increasing with the riskiness of the new sector. Consider a mean preserving spread of the asset return, leaving expected return qR unchanged. Such a spread reduces probability of success q but increases the return R of the project, and so raises the asset price P_X.

As Allen and Gale (2000a) argue, innovators receive an information rent when the banks cannot monitor. In the setup here, depositors supplying funds inelastically have to bear the cost. All the rent is captured by the owners of the scarce resource (the bubble is equal to the information rent). More generally, investors will get part of the rent via higher return to equity. In this section we demonstrated the key insight by Allen and Gale using the simplest setup. We assumed that banks are not able to monitor how investors allocate their funds across the two sectors. Inefficient monitoring should best be seen as a simple representation of weak financial intermediation. When weak intermediation allows agents to transfer part of the risk to other agents in the economy, there will be excessive risk taking and bubbles.

Take, as an example, the East Asian crisis, which frequently has been blamed on inefficiencies in the financial sector (possibly supplemented by implicitly relying upon a government guarantee to cover potential losses). The recent bubbles following Ponzi-game schemes in Albania and Rumania confirm the relevance of this argument. According to conventional wisdom, however, Western economies are characterized by highly efficient financial markets, designing sophisticated mechanisms to cope with monitoring problems. Nevertheless, plenty of real world examples demonstrate the role of lax intermediation in creating bubbles even in these sophisticated economies. Recent evidence following the failure of many new economy firms points to a serious distortion in the incentive structure for control (a prominent example being the Enron case).

Obviously efficient regulation of financial markets is a key element for preventing bubbles. Rather than assigning a task for monetary policy, this suggests that there is a great need for improving regulation and supervision to ensure efficient monitoring. In the remaining part of the chapter, we will consider the extent to which monetary policy can create a bubble. For that purpose we abstract from irrational exuberance and inefficient monitoring. So from now on, we will assume that banks are able to control investors' exposure to risk. First, we show how no bubble arises in this case.

6.2.5 No Bubble under Efficient Monitoring
When banks can control to what extent investors are exposed to the risky sector, they will charge a risk-adjusted rate of return. For all funds invested in the new economy, the rate depends on the amount of equity invested by the creditor herself. Let $D = P_X - E$ be the debt exposure in the economy. Under efficient monitoring, for $C < D(1+r)$ the bank will charge a risk adjusted rate of return defined as

$$qD(1+\hat{r}) + (1-q)C = D(1+r);$$

that is, for $C > D(1+r)$, lending is riskless as debt payments can be financed out of collateral, and so $\hat{r} = r$. As the arbitrage condition the gross return in the new economy sector has to equal the gross return in the old economy:

$$qR + (1-q)C - q(1+\hat{r})[P_X - E] - (1-q)C$$
$$= qR + (1-q)C - (1+r)[P_X - E] = (1+r)E,$$

or

$$P_X = P_X^* = \frac{qR + (1-q)C}{1+r}.$$

Clearly, under efficient bank monitoring, as the credit rate is adjusted properly to the risk involved, the real bubble disappears, and the asset price equals the fundamental value. We are back in the world of the Modigliani-Miller theorem.[7]

6.3 Financial Stability Concerns—Bubbles and Monetary Policy

In this section we analyze under what conditions central bank's concern for financial stability may contribute to a bubble. In concentrating on this aspect, we abstract from risk mechanisms like irrational behavior and monitoring problems.[8] We present a highly stylized benchmark model with a simple micro structure capturing the risk of financial disruption.

6.3.1 Restructuring under Bank Monitoring

We now modify the setup of the model presented in section 6.2 by introducing liquidation costs, making banks susceptible to runs. As in Diamond and Rajan (2000), banks play two important roles in the economy: First, they offer deposit contracts with nominal claims allowing for early withdrawal of funds. For simplicity, we do not model the demand for deposit contracts but simply take them as given. Traditionally the reason for these contracts is said to be the provision of liquidity insurance, as in Diamond and Dybvig (1983) or Allen and Gale (2000b). Diamond and Rajan (2000) present a quite different, equally relevant motivation for deposit contracts: under relationship lending a fragile structure is necessary to prevent banks from extracting private rents arising from their specific skills.

Second, banks monitor the firms they give loans to. Failing projects have a low liquidation value L if liquidated early. A share α of the failed projects, however, could recover a continuation value $C > L$, in case

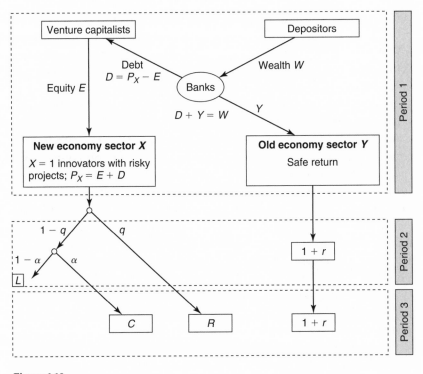

Figure 6.10
The basic model.

they were allowed to be restructured. Such restructuring requires replacement of management and monitoring by experts. When a firm gets into trouble, only its house-bank is capable to judge whether restructuring is worthwhile and to monitor the process of restructuring. When banks are forced into bankruptcy, however, this expertise is lost, and all firms are liquidated.

The structure of the model is outlined in figure 6.10. We now consider three periods. In the first period, funds are allocated across the two sectors just as in section 6.2. In the new economy sector, successful projects yield a return R in the final period. In the second, interim period 2, however, agents get a (fully informative) signal. It indicates the new economy projects that are about to fail. If these bad firms were forced to early liquidation during the interim period, they can only recover the liquidation value L. In contrast, if these firms are restructured rather than liquidated, they may recover the continuation value C in the final period.

Without monitoring, however, firms can recover C only with low probability β, but they will end up with no return at all (0) otherwise. We assume $\beta C < L$, so it will be inefficient to let the firms survive without restructuring. The managers, however, have an incentive to continue operation, in a gamble to resurrect their firms.

In contrast, due to its expertise out of relationship lending, the house-bank can distinguish among firms that should be closed down and those for which restructuring would be profitable. The latter (representing a share α of all failing firms) can recover the continuation value C provided that they are monitored by their house-bank. So under efficient restructuring, the average return of failing firms will be $\bar{C} = \alpha C + (1 - \alpha)L$. Only the bank has the knowledge and experience to restructure such a firm, by replacing the old management and monitoring the firm's performance until the final period. As in Diamond and Rajan (2000) the fragile financial structure (giving depositors the right to withdraw their funds in the intermediate period) prevents banks from extracting rents from their special skills due to relationship lending. Disruption of financial intermediation would lead to aggregate losses equal to $\bar{C} - L = \alpha(C - L)$.

The setup is meant to capture key elements of financial vulnerability: (1) the bank liabilities are characterized by deposit contracts, fixed in nominal terms, (2) banks as financial intermediaries invest in illiquid risky long-term assets, (3) early liquidation is costly, as the continuation value C exceeds the liquidation value L, and (4) disruption of financial intermediation destroys valuable information capital.[9] As shown below, the difference $C - L$ plays a crucial role in the analysis. $C - L$ should best be interpreted as the degree of financial fragility of the economic system arising from forced disruption, rather than as simple liquidation costs of individual firms.

6.3.2 The Case of Idiosyncratic Risk

We distinguish between two types of risk: idiosyncratic risk of individual firms and aggregate risk. For simplicity, we split the failure probability $1 - q$ in two parts:

$$1 - q = s + (1 - s - q).$$

With probability $(1 - s - q)$, the failure is due to pure idiosyncratic risk. A constant share $(1 - s - q)$ of new economy firms is affected by the shock. Due to the law of large numbers, there is no uncertainty about aggregate resources. In this case, where firms are allowed to restructure, expected aggregate returns paid to the bank are exactly equal to the nominal value A of claims of depositors:

$$A = Y(1 + r) + qD(1 + \hat{r}) + (1 - q - s)\bar{C}.$$

From the aggregate first-period budget constraint we know that

$$Y = W - (P_X - E) = W - D.$$

Furthermore, under efficient monitoring, $D(1 + r) = qD(1 + \hat{r}) + (1 - q)\bar{C}$. So A simplifies to

$$A = W(1 + r).$$

In the absence of an aggregate shock, aggregate returns flowing to the banks are equal to the nominal value of deposits. So banks are solvent, being able to pay back all depositors. As long as there is only purely idiosyncratic risk, no liquidity problem arises. There is no reason for depositors to run as they can all safely cash in their deposit in period 3 to get the real return originally contracted for. Thus banks will not recall loans to those firms for which the value as a going concern exceeds the liquidation value. There is no costly disruption of long-term investment.

6.3.3 Aggregate Shocks and Financial Fragility

With probability s an aggregate shock hits the whole new economy sector, with all firms failing. Now the economy runs into a serious problem.[10] When there are bad news about the aggregate prospective returns in the new economy, banks will not be able to pay out all depositors. Whenever, in the intermediate period 2, depositors get a signal that aggregate return will be less than the nominal claims of the deposit, they all have an incentive to run. This coordination problem results in costly inefficient liquidation of long-term assets, possibly aggravated by externalities involved. Injection of aggregate liquidity could avoid a default of the banking sector. As long as the continuation value of the economy exceeds liquidation value, public provision of aggregate liquidity may prevent costly disruption.

Debt exposure in the economy is characterized by $D = P_X - E$. As long as investors have enough own funds (high-equity finance) such that gross debt can be repaid even with early liquidation (i.e., $L > D(1 + r)$), financial fragility is no problem. For low-credit exposure of financial intermediaries, there is no need for intervention. For $L < D(1 + r)$, two cases have to be distinguished. First, we briefly discuss the case $D(1 + r) < \bar{C}$. That is the case with illiquid, yet solvent banks: aggregate expected return under efficient restructuring exceeds debt payments. Early liquidation triggered by a bank run would disrupt an inherent solvent economy. As in Diamond and Dybvig (1983), in the absence of intervention, there always exists a self-fulfilling equilibrium in which all depositors run. But we consider that case as being rather artificial. It can simply be eliminated by assertion of the central bank that it will be ready to provide enough liquidity. The announcement itself would be sufficient to prevent a run.

The much more interesting case is a debt exposure so high that the banking system would be insolvent even when allowing for the restructuring of new economy firms (i.e., those firms that could recover C are allowed to survive rather than liquidated). From now on, we assume that $D(1 + r) > \bar{C}$, which implies, of course, $D(1 + \hat{r}) > \bar{C}$.

6.3.4 Bubbles and Liquidity Provision

Whenever depositors observe an aggregate shock in period 1, indicating that the whole new economy sector is failing, a run on the banks will set in. A breakdown of the financial system will destroy the information capital built up by the banks via relationship lending and thus force all firms to early inefficient liquidation. This can only be prevented, if the central bank is willing to provide sufficient aggregate liquidity. The central bank has to inject enough liquidity such that banks are able to satisfy liquidity demand of depositors. Following Allen and Gale (2000b), we model this process such that in the event of a bank run, the central bank issues nominal claims to the banks, requiring that the money be paid back in the last period.

In the absence of liquidity injection, the price level in the economy is normalized to $p = 1$. As in Allen and Gale (2000b), liquidity injection raises the price level in the economy, thus reducing the real value of nominal debt: $[D(1 + \hat{r})]/p < D(1 + \hat{r})$ whenever $p > 1$. To avoid disruption of the system, the central bank has to provide enough liquidity to eliminate the risk of a run on banks. There is no incentive for depositors to run on banks when the liquidation value L of new economy firms is sufficient to repay the nominal value of their claims. Thus, to eliminate any risk of a general bank run, the price level will have to rise up to

$$\frac{D(1 + \hat{r})}{p} = L.$$

Since inflation reduces the real value of nominal debt, all restructured firms enjoy capital gains whenever inflation erodes the nominal value of the firm's debt such that real repayment is less than the continuation value of the firm:

$$\frac{D(1+\hat{r})}{p} < C$$

When investors rationally anticipate these capital gains, the asset price is driven up, ex ante, above the fundamental value. This way, financial stability concerns create a bubble equal to the expected present value of capital gains out of central bank's rescue operations. Thus the bubble is equal to the present expected value of this subsidy. The expected bubble is rising with the crash probability s and the firm's real return out of the central bank's rescue operation. As in sections 6.2.2 and 6.2.3, the bubble raises the asset price above its fundamental value:

$$B = P_X - P_X^* = s\alpha \frac{1}{1+r}\left(C - \frac{D(1+\hat{r})}{p}\right).$$

In the model the inefficiency caused by the bubble is represented by the output loss in the old economy sector. It is exactly equal to the bubble component B. The central bank has to trade off the cost of a rescue operation (the bubble created by moral hazard) against the risk associated with the disruption of financial intermediation. The expected gain of avoiding the breakdown of the financial system is captured by two elements: first, the difference between continuation and liquidation value $C - L$ for the share α of successfully restructured firms, given the aggregate shock. Second, contagion effects spilling over to other sectors in the economy. The costs of these spillovers are likely to rise with the fragility of the economic system, so we assume that spillover costs S are proportional to $C - L$, the costs of disruption of financial intermediation:

$$S = \gamma(C - L).$$

Ex ante, expected gains amounts to

$$G = s\alpha \frac{1}{1+r}(C - L + S) = s\alpha \frac{1+\gamma}{1+r}(C - L).$$

Gains exceed costs if $G - B > 0$, that is, if

$$G - B = s\alpha \frac{\gamma}{1+r}(C - L) > 0.$$

Whereas the direct benefits from preventing disruption of financial intermediation are exactly offset by the inefficiencies caused by the bubble, it will be rational for central banks to inject liquidity in a crisis whenever there is the risk of spillover effects arising from the disruption of financial intermediation.

6.4 Conclusions and Extensions

The chapter has modeled the link between financial fragility, asset markets, and monetary policy. It showed that central bank's concern about the cost of financial disruption generates an asymmetric response, thus contributing to the creation of an asset price bubble. In an economy with a highly leveraged financial structure, the central bank has an incentive to prevent a "run" on financial intermediation by injecting liquidity when asset values fall significantly. The inflationary side effect of this policy, reducing the real value of nominal debt, is what gives rise to a "put option" for investors. Leveraged investors, rationally anticipating this liquidity injection, drive asset prices above their fundamental values. The chapter showed that it is rational for central banks to inject liquidity in a crisis, whenever there is the risk of spillover effects arising from the disruption of financial intermediation.

The model characterized the central bank's policy, assuming that it has precise control about provision of liquidity. In view of the uncertainty about the transmission mechanism, which is especially high during a crisis, there may be good reasons to provide even more liquidity than actually needed. So the central banks concern about avoiding the breakdown of the financial system may make it more cautious to reduce liquidity once the crisis is on retreat. To avoid a severe breakdown, the central bank is likely to err on the safe side. The experience after the crash in 1987 confirms this view. Such an asymmetric response aggravates the moral hazard problem.

The results of this chapter illustrate the need to think about policy alternatives that reduce exposure to financial fragility right from the beginning, and so attack the problem at its source. Certainly careful regulation of financial markets is an important step in this direction. One way to reduce exposure is the control of the leverage ratio via margin requirements. Such a policy, however, would come at the cost of rationing investment in the new economy. Whenever the risk of an aggregate shock is small compared to potential benefits of the new economy sector, this option is inferior. Then, provision of aggregate liquidity (antideflationary policy) to prevent financial disruption is the superior policy response, even if it comes at the expense of creating a bubble out of moral hazard.

In view of the dominance of bank credit in the euro area, the risk of disruption of financial intermediation was modeled as a bank run. As Davis (2000) argues, the Diamond and Dybvig (1983) model may also be applied to securities markets. In the same way as runs on banks, there may be runs on security markets. Just like depositors, bond holders have a need for liquidity insurance and so prefer liquid markets. The coordination problem of depositors is simply replaced by a coordination problem among debt holders, so the mechanism worked out in the chapter may also be applied to the financial structure in the United States. A stock market crash triggering a credit crunch will result in disruption of financial intermediation when the economy is characterized by high-debt exposure. Independent of the specific financial structure, the key issue is leverage. Nevertheless, there are significant differences in financial structure. For example, there is no equivalent to relationship lending in the bond market, and so incentives for restructuring may be quite different. Furthermore, contagion effects may work quite differently. Historic evidence seems to suggest that financial fragility is of more serious concern in financial systems based on securities markets. A comparison between the different structures is a promising future research area.

Notes

I would like to thank Charles Goodhart, Korbinian Ibel, Ulrich Klüh, Axel Lindner, Adam Posen, and an anonymous referee for comments on previous versions of the chapter, as well as to seminar participants at the CESifo conference on Issues regarding European Monetary Union, the Technical University in Vienna, the 2001 European Meeting of the Econometric Society in Lausanne, the EEA meeting 2001 in Lausanne and the 2001 meeting of the Verein für Socialpolitik in Magdeburg.

1. Monetary policy, however, first has to solve a much deeper problem: to identify what type of information is driving changes in asset prices. This is essentially a signal extraction problem about the type of shocks. If asset prices are rising as a consequence of good news signaling a permanent positive supply shock with substantially improved growth potential, say in the new economy sector, there may be no inflationary pressure at all, and so no need to react. If, on the other hand, rising prices are the result of a pure bubble generated in the financial sector, it may indicate both inflationary pressure from short-run wealth effects and the risk of high volatility when the bubble will burst eventually in the

future, both calling for strong reactions. Again, things may be quite different when private agents adjust to the presence of a bubble by dampening consumption and limiting exposure to credit expansion (see Cogley 1999; Smets 1997).

2. See Smets (1997), Issing (1998), and Cogley (1999). One problem is that it may be too late to act without triggering a crisis when the bubble becomes evident. Take the crash in 1929 for instance. It is often cited that a policy of easy money before the crash contributed to the bubble, since the Fed failed to take deliberate action to prick the bubble. But as shown by Cogley (1999), starting in 1928, the Fed shifted toward increasingly tight monetary policy, motivated in large part by a concern about speculation in the stock market. The depth of the contraction had much to do with the fact that the Fed continued a tight money policy after the crash, in an attempt to contain the inflation.

3. As bubbles may burst as a result of bad news about aggregate shocks to the economy, in this chapter, we analyze such a case. We show that concerns about stability is a separate factor contributing to a bubble. A modified Taylor rule would be of no help in this case.

4. Of course, in reality, asset prices are driven by a combination of all three mechanisms. So Miller et al. (2000) argue that the Fed's policy has the effect to give each investor on the stock market the (false) impression of providing a put option that allows him to get out before the stock market crashes. Effectively Miller et al.'s model does nothing more than assume overconfidence in the Fed. They do not analyze central bank behavior at all.

5. In section 6.3, where we analyze the risk of runs, early liquidation of projects is assumed to be costly. The liquidation value is below the continuation value: $L < C$.

6. It would be straightforward to generalize the results to an economy with endogenous supply of new economy projects. Then any bubble will also produce an excess supply of risky projects above the efficient level.

7. Of course, principal agent problems may prevent the first-best solution. But when banks as principals choose the optimal monitoring technology (incentive compatible contracts to cope with moral hazard of investors), a second-best outcome will be obtained. It is likely to be characterized by constraining investment in the risky sector (like credit rationing) rather than overinvestment.

8. These factors would aggravate the problem, the same as would overexpansion of bank credit arising from relaxed lending standards out of euphoria.

9. When financial intermediation is disrupted, information capital is destroyed with possibly serious long-term impact, as the experience in Japan during the last decade illustrates. The losses are aggravated by spillover effects to other institutions with similar exposure. The stronger the exposure within the financial system, the stronger are these effects. So the failure of an intermediary is likely to generate externalities, triggering cascade effects across intermediaries. Incorporating these contagion effects into the model promises to be an important extension in future research.

10. Capital requirements and bank's equity could help smooth small aggregate shocks. In a drastic simplification, we intentionally introduce a large aggregate shock such that banks cannot take precautionary actions. It future work, the impact of capital requirements will be analyzed in a generalized framework with continuous rather than discrete shocks.

References

Allen, F., and D. Gale. 2000a. Bubbles and crises. *Economic Journal* 110: 236–56.

Allen, F., and D. Gale. 2000b. Optimal currency crises. *Carnegie Rochester Conference Series* 53(1): 177–230.

Batini, N., and E. Nelson. 2000. When the bubble bursts: Monetary policy rules and foreign exchange market behavior. Bank of England, London.

Bernanke, B. S., and M. Gertler. 1999. Monetary policy and asset price volatility. In *Federal Reserve Bank of Kansas City Economic Review* (4th quarter): 17–51.

BIS. 2000. Bank for International Settlements. 70th Annual report. BIS, Basel.

Bundesbank. 2000. The market for venture capital in Germany. *Monthly Bulletin*, Frankfurt, October.

Cecchetti, S. G., H. Genberg, J. Lipski, and S. Wadhwani. 2000. Asset prices and central bank policy. *Geneva Reports on the World Economy*. ICMB and CEPR, Geneva.

Cogley, T. 1999. Should the Fed take deliberate steps to deflate asset price bubbles? *Federal Reserve Bank of San Francisco Economic Review* 1: 42–52.

Davis, E. P. 2000. Financial stability in the euro area—Some lessons from US financial history. LSE Financial Markets Group Special Paper 123.

Diamond, D., and P. Dybvig. 1983. Bank runs, deposit insurance and liquidity. *Journal of Political Economy* 91: 401–19.

Diamond, D., and R. Raghu. 2000. A theory of bank capital. *Journal of Finance* 55: 2431–65.

Dornbusch, R. 1999. Comment on Bernanke/Gertler "Monetary Policy and Asset Price Volatility." In *Federal Reserve Bank of Kansas City Economic Review* (4th quarter): 129–35.

ECB. 2000. Asset prices and banking stability. Report prepared by the Banking Supervision Committee, Frankfurt.

Gertler, M., M. Goodfriend, O. Issing, and L. Spaventa. 1998. Asset prices and monetary policy: Four views. London: CEPR.

Greenspan, A. 1999. New challenges for monetary policy. Speech at Jackson Hole conference on New Challenges for Monetary Policy. August 27.

Hackethal, A., and R. H. Schmidt. 2000. Financing patterns: Measurement concepts and empirical results. Goethe University, Frankfurt. Working Paper, Finance and Accounting.

Miller, M., P. Weller, and L. Zhang. 2002. Moral hazard and US stock market: Analysing the "Greenspan put." *Economic Journal* 112: 171–86.

Schmidt, R. H., A. Hackethal, and M. Tyrell. 1997. Disintermediation and the role of banks in Europe: An international comparison. Goethe University, Frankfurt. Working Paper, Finance.

Smets, F. 1997. Financial asset prices and monetary policy: Theory and evidence. BIS Working Paper 47.

Comment on Chapter 6

Philippe Bacchetta

The burst of the stock market bubble in 2001 to 2002 is raising important policy issues. In particular, the problem is to find the appropriate monetary policy response as a bubble develops and after it bursts. Should the Federal Reserve have raised the interest rate when the 'irrational exuberance' was leading to ever increasing share prices in the late 1990s? Should the European Central Bank have followed the Fed in cutting interest rates after the fall in share prices? The opinions diverge on these issues. For example, Bernanke and Gertler (1999) argue that it is best to ignore asset price inflation since it is difficult to identify a bubble as it occurs. Others like Cecchetti et al. (2000) think that the central bank should directly target asset prices.

Illing joins this discussion and also touches on several other issues. A major question asked is whether monetary policy can alone create a stock market bubble by being passive in the upward phase in share prices, while being more expansionary after the downfall. Interestingly this is precisely the policy that the Fed appears to have followed in recent years. So the question is: Did the Federal Reserve create the stock market bubble in the late 1990s? In reality, there are obviously other factors, but the role of monetary policy in the stock market bubble is definitely an important question that is receiving growing attention. The analysis of Illing is therefore a welcome contribution to the debate.

Before considering monetary policy, the chapter examines a set of other factors that can lead to a bubble, such as irrational exuberance or weak financial intermediation. The analysis is based on a model by Allen and Gale (1998, 2000) that is an extension of Diamond and Dybvig (1983)'s model, which introduces aggregate shocks. Even though the model is highly stylized, it provides a precise framework with solid micro foundations of financial intermediation. The other advantage of this framework is that it is well known and has been used by a large number of authors.

The main contribution of Illing, however, is the analysis of monetary policy and share prices in section 6.3. In the model of that section, firms can go bankrupt if a bad shock hits the economy. If this occurs, depositors may run on banks as they realize that banks are making losses on their loans and may not be able to repay all creditors. Thus the banking system may collapse. Consequently the central bank finds it desirable to inject liquidity to save both firms and the banking sector. Illing shows that this intervention can lead to an asset price bubble.

How is a bubble created by this contingent monetary action? Through debt deflation! The injection of liquidity creates inflation so that the nominal value of firms' debt is reduced. This can offset the potential loss produced by the negative shock, especially when firms are highly leveraged. This type of subsidy contingent on bad shocks obviously increases the value of firms. Illing defines the bubble as the difference between the firms' values with and without subsidy.

Can we thus conclude that the lowering of interest rates by the Federal Reserve in the fall of 2002 is responsible for the stock market bubble in the 1990s? In my view, the answer is clearly no, and this chapter has not changed my view, as I find that the mechanism proposed is not convincing and does not apply to recent events. First, a bubble is a phenomenon that occurs over time. To explain a growing bubble following the logic of the chapter, it would be necessary to have an increasing probability of liquidity injection. The model does not tell us why this probability would increase. Second, the definition of a bubble is questionable. A bubble is typically considered as a deviation from the value justified by fundamentals. But isn't monetary policy one of the most important fundamentals in the macroeconomy?

A third issue is the mechanism of transmission of monetary policy, through debt deflation, that appears unrealistic. In particular, it assumes that prices are fully flexible in the short run so that inflation immediately follows a monetary injection. Actually prices should be changed more quickly than nominal interest rates. Moreover the model assumes that depositors are myopic so that monetary policy operates through a redistribution between depositors and firms: what firms gain by debt deflation is lost by depositors. They are myopic in the sense that equity owners can anticipate future monetary policy actions but not depositors. If they anticipated potential future inflation as well, they would ask for a higher nominal interest rate, which would have the bubble disappear. These are two crucial assumptions that are not even mentioned in the text. Unfortunately, this type of situation, where the microeconomics foundations are fully spelled out while the macro-economic assumptions are only implicit, is common. In these contexts it is premature to draw policy conclusions before verifying the main assumptions, in particular, regarding the monetary transmission channel.

Finally, the analysis relies on *debt* deflation, which is irrelevant for the current situation of *price* deflation. There is no sign whatsoever that inflation will increase in the years after the share prices decline. This is precisely the absence of inflation threat that has allowed the Fed to lower its interest rate. Ironically there is more threat of price deflation than price inflation after an asset price bubble. This was clearly illustrated by the Japanese experience in the recent decade. While the impact of monetary policy in the rising phase of share prices is still an open issue, it remains to be shown that the anticipation of monetary policy in the declining phase can have any impact.

References

Allen, F., and D. Gale. 1998. Optimal financial crises. *Journal of Finance* 53, 1245–1284.

Allen, F., and D. Gale. 2000. Bubbles and crises. *Economic Journal* 110: 236–56.

Bernanke, B. S., and M. Gertler. 1999. Monetary policy and asset price volatility. In *Federal Reserve Bank of Kansas City Economic Review* (4th quarter): 17–51.

Cecchetti, S. G., H. Genberg, J. Lipski, and S. Wadhwani. 2000. Asset prices and central bank policy. *Geneva Reports on the World Economy*. ICMB and CEPR, Geneva.

Diamond, D., and P. Dybvig. 1983. Bank runs, deposit insurance and liquidity. *Journal of Political Economy* 91: 401–19.

Index